An Introduction
to Anselm's Argument

An Introduction to Anselm's Argument

Gregory Schufreider

The King's Library

Philosophical Monographs
Second Annual Series

Temple University Press
Philadelphia

Library of Congress Cataloging in Publication Data

Schufreider, Gregory.
    An introduction to Anselm's argument.

    (Philosophical monographs)
    Includes bibliographical references and index.
    1. Anselm, Saint, Abp. of Canterbury, 1033-1109.
Proslogium.   2. God—Proof, Ontological.
I. Anselm, Saint Abp. of Canterbury, 1033-1109.
Proslogium. Selections. 1978.   II. Title.
III. Series: Philosophical monographs
(Philadelphia, 1978-   )
B765.A84S29   231′.042   78-15721
ISBN 0-87722-133-2
ISBN 0-87722-129-4 pbk.

Temple University Press, Philadelphia 19122
©1978 by Temple University. All rights reserved
Published 1978
Printed in the United States of America
ISSN 0363-8243

In Memoriam

Joseph Schufreider

1903-1977

. . .der Vater aber liebt,
Der über allen waltet,
Am meisten, dass gepfleget werde
Der veste Buchstab, und bestehendes gut
Gedeutet.

Hölderlin

Contents

Acknowledgments

This work was begun while I was a Church Fellow at the University of California, Santa Barbara (1973-74) and was completed during my stay as a Taft Post-doctoral Fellow at the University of Cincinnati (1976-77). I am pleased to be able to acknowledge my gratitude for this assistance. Most importantly, however, I would like to thank Paul Wienpahl—for everything.

Preface

In recent years, there has been as much confusion about the nature and identity of Anselm's argument as there has traditionally been dispute over its validity. Such confusion, I believe, reflects the fact that, from its inception to the present day, Anselm's own argument has never been properly understood and, despite all the notoriety it has received, has passed unnoticed. Finding our way to an argument which has been concealed under so many years of controversy and misunderstanding demands we follow an elusive path, and this work rests on the supposition that Anselm's text is the only reliable guide. My aim, then, is *to bring the reader into direct contact with the original argument*. This obviously cannot be accomplished through a mere presentation of the text, but requires a careful interpretation, the broad outlines of which I shall supply shortly. Before that, however, some preliminary remarks are in order which may begin to clarify the present philosophical situation with regard to Anselm's argument and in so doing demonstrate why a study of this sort is called for.

In what situation do we find Anselm's argument today? Certainly dispute over it is as acute as ever; and this would appear to be nothing new. Philosophers have been quarrelling over this argument since its "publication" and, of course, there is never anything new about controversy in philosophy. There is, however, something new about a kind of disagreement over Anselm's argument that reigns and has reigned in this century, especially in philosophy for the past fifteen years. The disagreement I have in mind is among not opponents but proponents of the argument, and it is not fundamentally over its validity but rather is a question of the argument's identity. And this is a relatively new development. The question of what the argument is, and where it is located in the text, has only recently become a central issue.

Historically, interpreters of Anselm simply assumed that his argument was contained in Chapter II of the *Proslogion*. This chapter alone was taken to be the crucial one, and it was this piece of reasoning that was later dubbed "the ontological argument." In 1960, however, a new sort of questioning was to be initiated by Norman Malcolm in his noted article "Anselm's Ontological Arguments."[1]   As the title suggests, Malcolm finds more than one ontological argument in the *Proslogion*. The first he finds in Chapter II, as the tradition had; but Malcolm finds another in Chapter III. He rejects the first and argues that the second is sound.

At this point, what is of interest is not the fairness of Malcolm's account so much as the effect it has had on discussions of Anselm. For in first opening up the problem of the identity of the argument, Malcolm put into question what previously had been treated as a settled matter. From this point on, no definitive interpretation of Anselm's argument could fail to take into consideration the problem of the relation of Chapter II to Chapter III and, in some way, come to grips with the question of what the argument is, whether there is more than one, and where it is located in the text. Quite independently of the value of Malcolm's account as an interpretation of Anselm, he is to be credited with forcing this question to be raised.

Since the appearance of Malcolm's article, there have been offered at least two other accounts of the identity of Anselm's argument which are worthy of our attention. The first of these was argued by D. P. Henry[2] and the other, more recently, by Richard La Croix.[3]   While both of these philosophers find a single argument for the existence of God, they find it in different places; that is, in effect, each finds a different argument. What those arguments are and how they differ from each other, and from Malcolm's, will be discussed in detail later.

Not only is it important to realize that there are presently at least three dominant and different accounts of what Anselm's argument is, but there is a more significant lesson in all this, and one that we must come to take seriously. In so far as these interpreters find different arguments, they also find Anselm to be showing different claims. This means that there is not only controversy over what Anselm's argument is, but consequently dispute over exactly what it purports to show. This is an issue whose full significance we may not sense, since it may be assumed from the start that we all know just what Anselm is after. Part of the burden of this study involves undercutting that assumption and demonstrating that the most crucial of all issues is what the argument (once we have understood what it is) claims to show and *how* it aims to provide a response to the question of the existence of God.

Today then, possibly more than at any other time, we greatly need to attempt to gain a clear understanding of the argument itself. What is still questionable is how such understanding can best be secured. I believe, as I have indicated, that there is only one course leading out of the present confusion and conflict. That course must be determined by a careful interpretation of the original text. There are, however, two very different ways in which one can endeavor to interpret a text. On the one hand, the interpreter can act as an elucidator, having as his aim bringing the text to light, while, on the other, an interpreter can act as a mediator who intervenes between text and reader. It is this latter approach to interpretation which is usually applied to Anselm. An interpreter will attempt to negotiate Anselm's argument with a 20th century mind, either by rendering it in a language more immediately palatable to the reader of today, or by applying "modern" developments to this age-old argument. Such an approach tends to give rise to new versions of the argument, and I think it fair to say that in this sort of case the interpreter is not so much interested in presenting Anselm's own argument as he is, so to speak, in salvaging it by means of some new version. In this way, the argument is presented to us, but mediated and altered.

We, on the other hand, are called upon to draw an argument from out of its concealment in obscurity, controversy, misunderstanding. Thus my account is basically expository; not, however, in a thoughtless sense of that term. My aim is not simply to repeat what is already evident, but to expose, to bring forth and into view that which has remained hidden from the start. Such interpretation is what is sometimes called hermeneutic or exegetic. The exegete is a guide who, rather than attempting to bring the argument to the reader as a negotiator would, attentps to direct the reader to the argument. To be sure, exposition as we understand it is a mode of interpretation, but one which has as its intent the explication of the text; the unfolding of it before the eye of a reader. In this way, there is no point in attempting to salvage the argument. The task is to display, not to defend it, unless that defense be against misunderstanding. In the end, if such interpretation is successful, the argument is left to speak for itself.

The way of interpreting, then, clings to the text, and only this sort of account of Anselm can lead us out of the confusion that abounds to-day concerning his argument. The interpretation I offer endeavors to bring the reader into direct contact with the argument, which can only be achieved through a careful scrutiny of the original text, giving special attention to Anselm's own words, to their systematic use and reuse. This demands a deliberate and methodical reading which moves through the text a step at a time, allowing us a first-hand grasp of the argument itself. Such a methodical movement through the text is undertaken in this study according to the following design.

In Chapter 1 I begin the analysis of Anselm's argument by develop-ing the reasoning of *Proslogion* II. For convenience, Chapter 1 is di-vided into three sections. The first deals with an interpretive exposition of the early stages of the argument, including the well-known *reductio* portion. In the second section, I break from this development in order to consider a certain classical misunderstanding which obscures what I take to be a modal dimension of the reasoning of II. Only when this misunderstanding is overcome can the conclusion of II be brought fully to view. In the final section, I complete the discussion by considering what this conclusion amounts to, and how it is intended to follow from the reasoning of II.

We find, however, that the conclusion of II does not bring us to the expressed aim of the argument, and so are forced to pursue its continu-ing development in Chapter 2 through a consideration of *Proslogion* III. Chapter 2 is also divided into three sections. The first deals with the *reductio* portion of III. In that section we find it is not at all clear how, or even if, the conclusion stated in III is intended to follow from this *reductio* alone. In the second section, then, the question of the relation of II to III must be posed and answered. A number of basic accounts of this relation are presented and criticized, and finally I offer an inter-pretation which seems to be suggested by a careful reading of the text. This interpretation results in the claim that what has been taken to be a separate proof for the existence of God in *Proslogion* II is no such thing, but instead is only the first stage in a single argument that spans II and III. The conclusion of this single argument, as well as the genuine significance of III is treated in the third and final section in view of my account of the relation of II to III.

Chapter 3 seeks to shed light on the most obscured aspect of Anselm's argument: *Proslogion* IV. On the basis of the conclusion of the single argument of II and III (i.e. on the basis of my account of Anselm's argument thus far) an aspect of this argument can be exposed which has been neglected by all previous interpreters. This dimension is crucial in that it speaks to the nature of the argument, how it is designed to function and what is intended to follow from it. By taking up discussion of Anselm's theory of signs, we are put in a position better to appreciate his understanding of the nature and function of reason, and consequently to see how the argument is to provide a rational response to the question of the existence of God. New issues, I think, are here raised concerning the very nature of Anselm's argument, issues which will finally lead to my conclusion.

In that Conclusion, I circle back to the beginning of the argument to complete the discussion by interpreting, on the basis of my treatment of II, III and IV, the opening line of II. I show that this opening line confirms from the beginning my account of the argument and is set there by Anselm as an interpretive hint which has never been heeded. At this point I am finally able to render plausible my contention that Anselm's argument has never been properly understood, and to explicate in what, fundamentally, such misunderstanding consists.

The body of this study, then, offers a step-by-step unfolding of Chapters II-IV of the *Proslogion* in which both traditional issues and as yet unappreciated aspects of Anselm's argument are investigated. With all the controversy, however, as to exactly where the argument is located, it may seem suspect to begin by assuming that the place to look for it is in Chapters II, III and IV. It must be admitted that this is assumed, at least initially. But it is well known that during Anselm's own lifetime these three chapters were extracted from the *Proslogion* and, with the affixture of the replies of Gaunilo and Anselm, circulated under the title: *Sumptum ex eodem libello*.[4] I take advantage of this hint about the original separation of these three chapters to begin with. I also accept the benefit of these replies wherever helpful. But my primary interest will center around Chapters II, III and IV. I will not be giving the replies any careful attention, except in so far as they shed light on these three chapters which were originally understood to be the *Ratio Anselmi*.

In the first instance, then, I shall move under this assumption and, in the final analysis, I shall offer no single argument to justify it. Only *the overall unity and completeness* of these three chapters, demonstrated by this entire study, finally serves as a basis for isolating Chapters II, III and IV from the rest of the *Proslogion* as Anselm's argument for the existence of God.

Despite the fact that everyone has read and judged some version of the ontological argument, it is my view that Anselm's argument has never received a fair hearing. All too often even those who speak in his name are more interested in giving some palatable version of the argument than in understanding Anselm's own. And there are countless convenient simplifications in circulation, none of which touch the heart of the argument. But we should not expect difficult matters to come to us so easily. The only manner in which we can reach Anselm's own argument is by making our way back to the original.

An Introduction
to Anselm's Argument

Chapter 1

Proslogion II

If we are to begin Chapter II of the *Proslogion* in the right way, then we must begin at the beginning. Strange as it may sound, this is an unusual place to commence a philosophical discussion of II; at least, this is not the point at which conventional interpreters tend to start. One rarely hears mention of the early part of this chapter at all, no doubt because, somehow, all of its earliest phases seem to be irrelevant to the argument proper, especially to its validity or invalidity. It is, however, in Chapter II that we are to begin to look for the argument, and there is little else we can do but deal with it in its entirety.

All chapters of the *Proslogion* begin with a title. It is known that these titles are not original, but that they are a later inclusion.[5] It is, however, also known that the titles were included by Anselm himself, supposedly for the convenience of the reader, and for the sake of clarity. The title of Chapter II runs:

Quod vere sit deus.

That God truly exists.[6]

One is safe in assuming that these chapter headings are announcements of something that is to be shown. Indeed, in this title, Anselm proclaims the project he is to attempt; that is, to show that: God truly exists. As we shall come to see, this chapter heading is of no little importance, and so I want to stress it from the start. For with this title Anselm declares himself. He has announced his intention to show that

3

God truly exists, and we must not rest content until he has offered us an argument that claims to show this, and exactly this. If he argues for anything less, he will have defaulted.

Now the chapter itself that follows this declaration begins with a short prayer that calls upon the Lord for help:

> *Ergo, domine, qui das fidei intellectum, da mihi, ut quantum scis expedire intelligam, quia es sicut credimus, et hoc es quod credimus.*

> Well then, Lord, You who give understanding to faith, grant me that I may understand, as much as You see fit, that You exist as we believe, and that You are that which we believe.

This opening line of II is normally ignored by philosophers. I suppose one would tend to think that the invocation is either rhetorical or merely an expression of Anselm the theologian and not properly a part of any argument he might give as a philosopher. To be sure, the form of address is religious; but this in no way suggests that it lacks philosophical content, nor that it can be dismissed out of hand as unimportant to his argument. Unfortunately, and this may help to account for its neglect, this opening line cannot be properly interpreted until the very end, that is to say, until after we have gained some understanding of the fullness of Anselm's argument. At this point, however, we can take note of one controversial issue surrounding it.

Among those who take the line seriously and seek its significance, rather than dismissing it as an adorning piece of rhetoric, there seems to be some question about the meaning of the last part. In Latin it reads:

> . . . *quia es sicut credimus, et hoc es quod credimus.*

This what Anselm seeks to understand. Now many have taken this petition to mark a dual propose operating in the *Proslogion* as a whole. On the one hand, so it has been argued, Anselm wants to prove that God exists (. . . *quia es sicut credimus* . . .) and on the other, he wants to show what God is (. . . *et hoc es quod credimus* . . .). Indeed, some interpreters have gone so far as to divide the *Proslogion* into separate parts, corresponding to this dual purpose: Chapters II-IV are said to be concerned with the existence of God, while Chapters V-XXVI are said to deal with the nature of God.[7] According to this view, there are two very different purposes separated out at the beginning of II. The first is to prove that God exists, the other to show what God is. And, of course, it is claimed that Anselm turns to the first of these in Chapter II.

I believe that the acceptance of this view is fatal to the profundity and completeness of Anselm's argument as it occurs in Chapters II-IV. Despite the fact that Anselm appears to bring out two different issues here, there is no suggestion, so far as I can see, that he intends to deal with one, and then the other. Once we have properly understood Chapter IV, I think it can be shown to be crucial that these issues are not separated. This, however, cannot be argued for until we have accomplished our discussion of the entire argument. At this level, all that can be said is that Anselm declares in the very beginning of II that he seeks to understand *both* that God exists as he believes *and* that God is that which he believes.   And we can fairly assume that this is what he is going to attempt to show. At what point, and in what way, he will attempt to show either or both of these are still open questions, and must remain so, at least until we can base a claim upon the text itself. I believe that we will be able to do this, once we have developed the argument of II, III and IV, but not until then. All we can do now is simply postpone further discussion of the matter until we have arrived at that point.

Such an arrival, however, depends upon our successfully making our way through the argument, and the line following the opening one actually sets us in motion toward that end:

Et quidem credimus te esse aliquid quo nihil maius cogitari possit.

And certainly we believe that You are something than which nothing greater can be thought.

The "You," of course, refers to God. He is said to be *aliquid quo maius nihil cogitari possit*. This strange and complex phrase designates the matter for thinking with which we will be dealing throughout Anselm's argument. Let us note, however, that the phrase is not a concoction of Anselm's. It is something that "we believe"; that is, something those of faith already have believed. Indeed, the exact phrase, as well as phrases very much like it, had occured throughout the tradition, from Augustine on.[8]   In other words, if one takes this as a definition of God, as many seem to, then clearly it is not a stipulative definition. Anselm has not introduced a new term. He has, if you will, reported on the usage of an established term by appealing to something "we believe" where the "we" refers to an entire tradition. In this sense, "something than which nothing greater can be thought" is more like a "revealed Name of God" than an arbitrary definition.[9]

Anselm's contribution lay not in the contrivance of a "do-all" phrase, but in his ability to exploit the fecundity of an already existing name of God. As important, then, as the demand to clearly think this phrase (which one might see as the project of the argument) is the need to understand the way in which its introduction figures into the argument itself. For this phrase forms the very foundation of Anselm's reasoning in that it supplies *a method of arguing*. Later we shall see how even a slight alteration of this key phrase changes the argument, and how Anselm responds to such a change. Without this phrase there is no argument, at least, not Anselm's own; and this is precisely why it is appropriate to refer to it as the "key" phrase. This, however, will not be completely clear until we have seen it in action, and come to appreciate the delicate moves Anselm is able to effect by means of it.

Nevertheless, the centrality of this phrase is reflected even in the manner in which the lead question of Chapter II is posed. For it is by means of the transition from "God" to "something than which nothing greater can be thought" that the main concern of II can be put in a form with which Anselm can handily deal:

> *An ergo non est aliqua talis natura, quia 'dixit inspipiens in corde suo: non est deus'?*

> Or can it be that a thing of such a nature does not exist, since 'the Fool has said in his heart, there is no God'?

This is the first mention of the question of the existence of God in II, and it is important to notice exactly how it is put. To do this, we must attend to Anselm's own words, for the English translation is distracting. The reason for this is that in the same sentence *"non est"* first is translated as "does not exist" and later as "there is no." The basis for this is no doubt literary: it sounds better not to repeat the "does not exist." But Anselm repeats himself. And this is no coincidence. For, in the original, a symmetry is suggested between "*non est aliqua talis natura*" and "*non est deus.*" In fact, it is precisely this correspondence that the sentence is intended to be stressing. With the "*aliqua talis natura*" direct reference is made to something of the nature of that than which nothing greater can be thought. At the same time, the line speaks of God, for the Fool says: "*non est deus.*" What is being stressed in this sentence is neither the "*deus*" nor the "*non est deus,*" but rather that because ("*quia*") the Fool has said in his heart that God does not exist, he must therefore ("*ergo*") be claiming that something of the nature of that than which nothing greater can be thought does not exist. And although the question mark at the end of the sentence follows the "*non est deus,*" it is evident that the clause in which this appears is not in the interrogative. Rather, that God does not exist is simply asserted as what the Fool has said in his heart. The fundamental question of this line, and the one that concerns us in Chapter II is: "*non est aliqua talis natura*?"

What is crucial for Anselm is the nature (of that) than which nothing greater can be thought. It is the claim that God is of such a nature that he emphasizes with this question. As it turns out, the lead question introduced in II really asks: Can it be that something than which nothing greater can be thought does not exist? And it is to this question that Anselm now turns. Since we have made the complete transition from "God" to "something than which nothing greater can be thought," everything that occurs in the argument from this point on occurs in the name of, and on the basis of, this key phrase. "God" will not return again until much later.

The lead question should guide us to the argument itself, for it is in response to this question that the reasoning proper begins. The first step that Anselm takes is to suggest that, in some way, the Fool understands the key phrase:

Sed certe ipse idem insipiens, cum audit hic ipsum quod dico: 'aliquid quo maius nihil cogitari potest', intelligit quod audit; et quod intelligit in intellectu eius est, etiam si non intelligat illud esse.

But surely, when this same Fool hears what I am speaking about, namely 'something than which nothing greater can be thought', he understands what he hears, and what he understands exists in his understanding, even if he does not understand that it exists.

The way in which the Fool understands the phrase is evident: he understands it in so far as he hears it, that is, he understands what he hears. I take this to mean that in so far as he speaks the language, and is not an idiot, he can understand this expression to some extent. For although the phrase is odd, it is not, so Anselm *assumes*, entirely unintelligible.

We must be very careful, however. In the above quotation, Anselm speaks of the Fool understanding what he hears, and, so we are told, in so far as it is understood, it exists in his understanding. Put in this way, it seems apparent that what is understood are the words "something than which nothing greater can be thought," for what is claimed is that the Fool understands what he hears. So, one might be tempted to conclude, what Anselm means is that the words exist in his understanding (as one might say that the sounds exist in his ear).

But, if we look closely at what is said, it will become strikingly evident that Anselm means no such thing. Here again, we must fix our attention on the Latin. The quotation marks around *aliquid quo maius nihil cogitari potest* are, of course, not original but interpolation. This makes it appear as if Anselm is talking about the words. Furthermore, in so far as, at this point, he claims that the Fool understands what he hears, this appearance may be secured. Nevertheless, if we look at what the entire line says, it becomes clear that we cannot be talking about the words alone. To be sure, Anselm begins by claiming that the Fool should be able to understand what he hears, and it is the words that he hears. Notice, however, that it is not enough that he hears them, he must also understand what he hears. Now, what is understood exists in the understanding. Is Anselm talking about the words here? Certainly not, for what he goes on to say is that what is understood exists in his understanding *even if he does not understand it to exist*. This "it" cannot refer to the words, for no one doubts that they exist. Rather, the "it" must refer to something than which nothing greater can be thought. It is this which the Fool understands (and so exists in his understanding) and yet does not understand to exist.

Admittedly it may be hard to tell what to make of this. It seems clear that the Fool hears the words, yet, it seems equally clear that what Anselm claims to exist in his understanding (even if he does not understand it to exist) are not the words but something than which nothing greater can be thought. Somewhere a shift has occurred: the words are what is heard, but in some sense, it must be the thing that is understood, and so exists in his understanding. One way to explain this would be to assume that Anselm held a principle, not uncommon to his time, like the following: if a word for (or a description of) X is heard and understood, then, in some sense, X is understood.[10]

Recognizing this move to be based on a claim something like the above may be a first step toward clarifying the strange but important claim that if the Fool understands something than which nothing greater can be thought, then it exists in his understanding. For although the Fool initially understands the words, nonetheless, it is not Anselm's view that it is the words that exist in his understanding. Rather, if in so far as the phrase "something than which nothing greater can be thought" is understood, something than which nothing greater can be thought is understood, then when Anselm says that what is understood exists in the understanding, he is talking about something than which nothing greater can be thought, and not the words.

This, however, may appear to raise certain difficulties. If it is not the words, but the object, which is understood and exists in the understanding, then it would seem that it has been assumed that there is such an object, in which case Anselm would be taking the circular path to proving that it exists.

The answer to this problem may help us to see not only what Anselm means when he speaks of something existing in the understanding, but may, in so doing, explain the move from "is understood" to "exists in the understanding." To begin with, we shall assume as settled that Anselm is claiming that what the Fool understands, but does not understand to exist, is something than which nothing greater can be thought, and not the words. But if it is the object, and not the words that is understood and exists in the understanding, and if Anselm's argument is not to beg the question from the start, then we cannot help but face the view that is beginning to emerge: Anselm thinks that something can be understood, not the words, but the thing, and as such be an object of understanding independent of whether or not the object exists in reality. Such an object of understanding exists in the understanding even if it is not understood to exist (in reality). Here, of course, "object" is being used in a very broad sense to refer to what exists in reality as well as what does not, just so long as it exists in the understanding.[11]   In order for something to be an object of understanding, to be inspected and analyzed by the understanding, we need not have decided the question of whether or not it exists in reality. Rather, if a word for (or a description of) X is understood, X is understood; if X is understood, then X is an object of understanding; and if X is an object of understanding, X exists in the understanding.[12]

Anselm's willingness to speak of something as an object or thing even if it does not exist in reality is manifest in the general claim that follows the line we have been discussing, a claim which is then carefully clarified by means of a concrete example. The general claim runs:

Aliud enim est rem esse in intellectu, aliud intelligere rem esse.

For it is one thing for an object to exist in the understanding, and another thing to understand that an object exists.

Here he uses the same word, *"res,"* to range over both what exists in the understanding, and so presumably might not exist in reality, as well as what is understood to exist. In this line, then, Anselm seems quite willing to call something a thing, (*"res"*) even before he knows that it exists, just so long as it exists in the understanding. And since something could exist in the understanding which did not exist in reality, apparently, in this case, Anselm would also call it a thing; that is, even if a thing does not exist in reality, nonetheless, in so far as it is understood, that thing exists in the understanding.

This general distinction is immediately explicated in terms of a concrete example, so let us look there for some assistance:

Nam cum pintor praecogitat quae facturus est, habet quidem in intellectu, sed nondum intelliget esse quod nondum fecit. Cum vero iam pinxit, et habet in intellectu et intelligit esse quod iam fecit.

Thus, when a painter plans beforehand what he is going to execute, he certainly has (the picture) in his understanding, but he does not yet understand that it exists because he has not yet executed it. However, when he has now painted it, he both has it in his understanding and he understands that it exists because he has now made it.

The general claim is given a certain precision through this example, for we see exactly in what sense it is one thing for something to exist in the understanding, and another for something to be understood to exist. We are presented with two cases: the unexecuted work, which the painter has in his understanding but does not understand to exist, and the executed work, which the painter both has in his understanding and understands to exist. Notice that existing in the understanding pertains to both cases under discussion. This tells us how, and in what sense, it is one thing to exist in the understanding and another to be understood to exist: to say that a thing exists in the understanding leaves open the question of whether or not it is understood to exist. For what exists in the understanding might just as well be understood to exist (executed work) as not understood to exist (unexecuted work). The phrase "*esse in intellectu*", then, is of such an order that it is itself neutral with respect to the question of existence.

There is another matter brought out by the painter-example which can be appreciated only if we realize that Anselm employs the notion of understanding in stronger and weaker senses. Gaunilo notices this in his second reply, and Anselm affirms it in his own response.[13] When, for example, we say that the Fool "understands what he hears", we mean this in the weakest sense of "understand" in which a merely cogitational activity is involved. But when we say of the executed work that it is "understood to exist," Anselm has a much stronger sense of "*intellegere*" in operation, and in this sense understanding does not merely involve cogitation, but the certainty of cognition. In this stronger sense, if something is understood to exist, then it exists.

This means that when we speak of something that both exists in the understanding and is understood to exist, we are speaking of something that exists both in the understanding and in reality. Furthermore (setting aside those cases in which something exists in the understanding but has not yet been determined to exist in reality while, in fact, it does) if something exists in the understanding but is not understood to exist, then it exists in the understanding alone. These phrases offered in the painter-example prefigure, and consequently illuminate, phrases to be employed later in the argument. So if it is one thing for something to exist in the understanding and another for it to be understood to exist, then analogously, it will be one thing for something to exist in the understanding and another for it to exist both in the understanding and in reality. What is more, in that Anselm treats the categories offered in the painter-example as exhaustive for his purposes—that is, anything that exists in the understanding is either understood to exist or not understood to exist—analogously, Anselm would certainly have held that, in principle, *whatever exists in the understanding either exists in the understanding alone or exists both in the understanding and in reality*. And it is this principle which figures significantly into the reasoning of II.[14]

Indeed, with this principle emerging out of the painter-example, it should be easier to see why:

> *Convincitur ergo etiam insipiens esse vel in intellectu aliquid quo nihil maius cogitari potest, quia hoc cum audit intelligit, et quidquid intelligitur in intellectu est.*

> Even the Fool, then, is forced to agree that something than which nothing greater can be thought exists in the understanding, since he understands this when he hears it, and whatever is understood exists in the understanding.

For even though the Fool must admit that he understands what he hears, in some weak sense, and so is forced to concede that something than which nothing greater can be thought exists in the understanding; he is in no way admitting that, in the strong sense, it is understood to exist. This becomes evident if we consider the general claim: Whatever exists in the understanding either exists in the understanding alone, or exists both in the understanding and in reality. To admit that something exists in the understanding leaves open either of two equal possibilities; for admitting that it exists in the understanding has not prejudiced the question of whether it exists in the understanding alone, or both in the understanding and in reality, and it is to this question that the argument now turns.

Anselm wastes no time in showing his hand, for the very next line declares:

> *Et certe id quo maius cogitari nequit non potest esse in solo intellectu.*

> And surely that than which a greater cannot be thought cannot exist in the understanding alone.

This is a powerful claim. Let us begin our inspection of this line by noticing two features of its surface appearance. To start with, Anselm, for the first time, changes "*aliquid quo nihil maius cogitari potest*" to "*id quo maius cogitari nequit.*" The "*id*" is translated "that" in order to indicate its substitution for "*aliquid*" ("something") in the key phrase. We should be aware that this "*id*" suggests sameness; indeed, it is the root of our English word "identity." Exactly how this change, which calls attention to the notion of identity, figures into the argument will become evident shortly.

The second change involves the substitution of "*nequit*" ("cannot") for "*nihil . . . potest*" in the key phrase. Why does Anselm make this change; that is, why does he not use "*potest*" here? The answer to that is to be found in the fact that he does use "*potest*," only not in the key phrase, but in what follows it, for precisely what he tells us is that this *id quo maius cogitari nequit*:

> . . . *non potest esse in solo intellectu* . . .

and I believe special attention in this sentence is meant to be given to the "*non potest.*" This use of "*potest*" is intended to express possibility, or in this case, impossibility ("*non potest*"). If we hold him to his word, Anselm is not saying that something than which nothing greater can be thought does not exist in the understanding alone, but that it cannot; that this is impossible. How or if he can show this, we will have to see. That this is what he intends to show is not only clearly stated, but emphasized by substituting "*nequit*" in the key phrase so that the "*potest*" of the last half of the line stands out. Notice in this connection that after this line, Anselm returns to the use of "*potest*" in the key phrase (except in the last line where he uses "*valet*") although he persists in using "*id*" (again, except in the last line) in the remainder of Chapter II.

This, then, is what Anselm wants to show:

> . . . that than which a greater cannot be thought *cannot* exist in the understanding alone.

And, as everyone knows, he intends to demonstrate this by means of a *reductio ad absurdum*. What is not always clear, however, is exactly what that *reductio* claims to show; that is, normally it is assumed it claims God exists, while it would seem more correct to assume that the *reductio* aims to show what this very line announces. How Anselm moves once this has been shown will have to be discussed later. For now, it is important not to confuse strategies. The reasoning we are about to inspect, in the next two crucial lines, is employed to show exactly what it claims to show: that something than which a greater cannot be thought cannot exist in the understanding alone. How this connects with what has gone before, and can be concluded from it, will also be discussed at an appropriate point. The project for the moment is to see how the argument attempts to show what it claims to be able to show.

Anselm begins by making this notorious suggestion:

Si enim vel in solo intellectu est, potest cogitari esse et in re, quod maius est.

For if it exists in the understanding alone even, it can be thought to exist in reality also, which is greater.

It is clear that there is some sort of contrast being made out in this line, but I don't think it is at all clear between what. The most apparent way of understanding it would be as pointing up the difference between what "exists in the understanding alone," and what "can be thought to exist in reality also." That, however, is precisely *not* what the contrast is set up to bring out. For if these are the right phrases that Anselm wants to be contrasting, then it would follow that what exists in the understanding alone cannot be thought to exist in reality, and it is doubtful that he wants to be saying this. It would seem rather that under the phrase "exists in the understanding alone" would be all those things that do not exist, and yet *can be thought* to exist in reality. For there are a great many things that exist in the understanding alone, and nonetheless can be thought to exist in reality; unexecuted paintings, for example, and it is evident that Anselm intends to include such things under his category *esse in solo intellectu*. It cannot be then, that because something "can be thought to exist in reality also" that it is greater than what exists in the understanding alone, because the fact that something can be thought to exist in reality is *not sufficient to distinguish it* from what exists in the understanding alone.

What, then, is Anselm aiming to contrast that actually is a contrast? The answer to that is as straightforward as it can be: he is contrasting what exists *"in solo intellectu"* with what exists *"et in re"* (*i.e., et in intellectu et in re*). This characterization, however, may seem inadequate since we need to understand the *"potest cogitari esse et in re"* as one element in the contrast, and I have neglected the *"potest cogitari"* in my account. Yet I believe this is essentially correct. This *"potest cogitari"* has no place in the *content* of the constrast. Instead, it belongs to the *form* of the argument. At this point we first encounter the unique method of arguing which *aliquid quo nihil maius potest cogitari* allows. This "can be thought" only belongs with the "exists in reality also" as a formal requirement of the procedure. Nonetheless, it is no idle matter, but should suggest the importance of the key phrase itself. For although the contrast is properly between what exists in the understanding alone and what exists both in the understanding and in reality, the requirement that this be in a form appropriate to something than which nothing greater can be thought makes it possible for us to assert this contrast without in any way assuming that something exists in reality. For all that has been claimed is that if one *can think*: something that exists in reality, they can think something greater than what exists in the understanding alone. And from this it follows that something greater *can be thought* than what exists in the understanding alone; but this is all that follows. Where it leads, we shall have to wait and see.

That this is what is being claimed here becomes more evident if we consult what Anselm has to say on this matter in a reply. Notice how it is put:

> *An enim si est vel in solo intellectu, non potest cogitari esse et in re? Aut si potest, nonne qui hoc cogitat, aliquid cogitat maius eo, si est in solo intellectu?*

> For if it exists in the understanding alone even, cannot it be thought to exist also in reality? And if it can, is it not the case that he who thinks this thinks something greater than it, if it exists in the understanding alone?[15]

When Anselm says: ". . . he who thinks this . . ." it seems obvious that he does not mean; he who thinks: it can be thought to exist in reality;

but rather, he who thinks: it exists in reality. But there is something else worth noticing here. What follows from this, and precisely what Anselm seems to be concerned with, is that ". . . he who thinks this *thinks of something greater*." In other words, what interests him is that something greater *can be thought* than what exists in the understanding alone. So that while Anselm assumes the general principle to the effect that if something exists both in the understanding and in reality, it is greater than what exists in the understanding alone, he aims to conclude from this only that something greater can be thought than what exists in the understanding alone, and this, of course, would be true even if nothing as a matter of fact existed; presuming, that is, the general principle he is invoking here is legitimate.[16]

The critical claim Anselm is making here is that something greater can be thought than what exists in the understanding alone. I stress this because it is important not to become fixated in the view that the sole issue is Anselm's suggestion that it is greater to exist in reality than in the understanding alone. He does, of course, make this latter claim, but only in an attempt to provide grounds for the former claim. It may be that other grounds could be provided, and so while the former claim is essential to Anselm's argument, the latter may not be. I do not intend to defend either claim, although I might say that the former seems to allow for a greater variety of defense.

In any event, given Anselm's adherence to the view that for any thing that exists in the understanding alone a greater can be thought, we should have already guessed how the *reductio* is to proceed:

Si ergo id quo maius cogitari non potest, est in solo intellectu: id ipsum quo maius cogitari non potest, est quo maius cogitari potest.

If then that than which a greater cannot be thought exists in the understanding alone, this same that than which a greater cannot be thought is that than which a greater can be thought.

The content of what Anselm is saying here should be obvious. In the case in point, what is claimed to exist in the understanding alone, is something than which a greater cannot be thought. But, in so far as we accept that something greater can be thought than what exists in the understanding alone, if something than which a greater cannot be thought exists in the understanding alone, it is something than which a greater can be thought. The Latin stresses this by not repeating the "*id*" in the last phrase ("*quo maius cogitari potest*"), but instead "doubling" it from the beginning with an "*id ipsum*," This *id ipsum* is employed to emphasize the notion of identity. For the last half of the sentence tells us that the very same being itself (*id ipsum*) is both that than which a greater can be thought and that than which a greater cannot be thought, *if* we assume that it exists in the understanding alone. Therefore, something must be held not to be the very same being that it itself is. As Anselm immediately informs us, this is clearly impossible:

Sed certe hoc esse non potest.

But this is obviously impossible.

He does not say that this is inaccurate or incorrect, but flatly, that it is impossible. The same being simply *cannot* be both something than which a greater cannot be thought and something than which a greater can be thought. For in order to be the one (e.g. something than which a greater can be thought) it must fail to be the other (something than which a greater cannot be thought). And if it is the one (i.e. something than which a greater cannot be thought) then it must fail to be itself, in order to be the other (something than which a greater can be thought). But, first and foremost, a thing must be itself; so the law of identity dictates.

That there is a modal character to Anselm's language is not only evident, but is also stressed in the Latin. In each case, *impossibility* is entailed by the attempt even to assume that something than which a greater cannot be thought exists in the understanding alone. Indeed, the very line that claims this to be impossible:

Sed certe hoc esse non potest.

is strikingly similar in form to the line that asserts what the *reductio* is to show:

Et certe . . . non potest esse in solo intellectu.

And although the "*hoc*" of the first quotation refers directly to the contradiction of the line immediately preceding it (". . . *id ipsum quo*

maius cogitari non potest est quo maius cogitari potest . . ."), it indi-
rectly refers to the opening clause that generates this contradiction:

> *Si . . . est in solo intellectu . . .*

In both cases, then, the impossibility referred to, either directly or indi-
rectly, is that something than which a greater cannot be thought exists
in the understanding alone. Repeatedly this is claimed to be impossible. What Anselm declares to follow from his *reductio*, then; what is
claimed to have been shown, and what his reasoning is designed to be
strong enough to show, is that something than which a greater cannot
be thought cannot exist in the understanding alone.

This point, as well as some others can be amplified if we pause for a
moment in the development of the reasoning of II in order to discuss an
argument which may be confused with Anselm's, and is not itself sufficient to sustain the strength of this conclusion. By contrasting this
misunderstanding with his own argument, we may be able better to
bring into prominence the unique force of Anselm's reasoning.

Almost as quickly as Anselm's argument was scribed and circulated,
it was misunderstood. The originator of this classical misunderstanding
of the argument was its first "interpreter" and well-known adversary,
Gaunilo.[17]   In some ways we should not be too hard on him, for his
version of the reasoning of II appears to be the result of an honest mistake. He simply misses the most crucial aspect of the argument, and
shows this quite blatantly in his own characterization of it. Gaunilo
thinks that Anselm reasons his way to the existence of God as follows:

> *. . . et hoc ita probatur maius est esse et in re quam in solo intellectu,
> et si illud in solo est intellectu, maius illo erit quidquid etiam in re
> fuerit, ac sic maius omnibus minus erit aliquo et non erit maius
> omnibus, quod utique repugnat . . .*

And this is proved by the fact that it is greater to exist both in the
understanding and in reality than in the understanding alone. For if
this same being exists in the understanding alone, whatever existed
also in reality would be greater than this being, and thus that which
is greater than everything would be less than some thing and would
not be greater than everything, which is obviously contra-
dictory . . .[18]

Anselm saw, in his response to this, that the whole argument as Gaunilo presents it could be put into a single line. Let us take notice of exactly what he has to say in his own defense:

> *Primus, quod saepe repetis me dicere, quia quod est maius omnibus est in intellectu, si est in intellectu est et in re—aliter enim omnibus maius non esset omnibus maius—nusquam in omnibus dictis meis invenitur talis probatio. Non enim idem valet quod dicitur 'maius omnibus' et 'quo maius cogitari nequit', ad probandum quia est in re quod dicitur.*

First, you often reiterate that I say that that which is greater than everything exists in the understanding, and if it exists in the understanding, it exists also in reality, for otherwise that which is greater than everything would not be that which is greater than everything. However, nowhere in all that I have said will you find such an argument. For 'that which is greater than everything' and 'that than which a greater cannot be thought' are not equivalent for the purpose of proving the real existence of the thing spoken of.[19]

Anselm is no less than emphatic in his reply: "Nowhere in all that I have said will you find such an argument." Now one may be tempted to say that the only reason Anselm disowns this argument is because Gaunilo has the key phrase wrong. He says "that which is greater than everything" while Anselm says "that than which a greater cannot be thought." So simply make the substitution and both Gaunilo and Anselm will be happy. Such a move is short-sighted, however, and this is indicated in the concluding line. For as we have already seen, it is this phrase that supplies what I called a method of arguing. If I am right about this, then if the phrase is altered, so is the procedure. In other words, if it may be put in these terms, in the case of this argument there is a special relation of form to content. One cannot alter the content of the key phrase without altering the form of the argument. We shall deal with this in a concrete fashion shortly. For now, let us say that there is much more going wrong in this version than a simple substitution that can be corrected by replacing the original phrase.

Exactly how this substitution alters the argument of Chapter II, Anselm does not tell us. Instead, immediately after claiming that

Gaunilo has made this change, he gets himself involved in a very complicated consolidation of the reasoning of Chapters II and III, in an attempt to offer an argument that will work with "something than which a greater cannot be thought," but will not work with "that which is greater than everything." I would not like to go into this argument here, but rather keep our eyes fixed on Chapter II, for it is Gaunilo's characterization of this argument that Anselm explicitly repudiates as being: ". . . nowhere in all that I have said . . .". Suffice to say that Anselm treats the substitution of his key phrase as no less than crucial. In what follows, I should like to be able to provide what Anselm did not, that is, an account which would show exactly how this substitution alters the reasoning of II, and on that basis speculate why Anselm would so strenuously object to Gaunilo's version of his argument.

I shall take a hint from Anselm, and begin by considering what the change in the key phrase amounts to by attempting to discern if, and in what way, a change in the phrase might require a change in the reasoning. Well, what is the difference between "something than which nothing greater can be thought" (*aliquid quo nihil maius cogitari potest*) and "that which is greater than everything" (*maius omnibus*)? On the surface, the answer seems evident: "that which is greater than everything" lacks the "can be thought" (*cogitari potest*), that is, these key words are omitted from Gaunilo's phrase, and are also omitted from his argument. At every point then at which these words figure critically into the reasoning, Gaunilo will have to alter the argument in order to fit with "that which is greater than everything" rather than with "something than which nothing greater can be thought."

There is one very obvious point at which this "can be thought" figures importantly into the argument, a point that we have already discussed. It is that point at which Anselm says:

> *Si enim vel in solo intellectu est, potest cogitari esse et in re, quod maius est.*

> For if it exists in the understanding alone even, it can be thought to exist in reality also, which is greater.

And if we left the "can be thought" out of this line, and slightly altered it so as to render it intelligible, it could be made to read:

> ... if it exists in the understanding alone, then assuming it exists in reality also, it would be greater ...

However, it is plain we cannot argue in this way, since in so formulating the matter precisely what would have to be assumed to exist in reality is that which is greater than everything. We must show that if it exists in the understanding alone it would be less than something; but this something cannot be itself, if it existed in reality, since just what is in question is whether it exists in reality or not.

Gaunilo does not make this mistake. He so modifies the line to read in a way that does not commit this obvious fallacy. What he says is that:

> ... if this same being exists in the understanding alone, whatever existed also in reality would be greater than this being, and thus that which is greater than everything would be less than some thing and would not be greater than everything.

Here Gaunilo claims that if that which is greater than everything exists in the understanding alone, it would be less than *anything* that existed in reality. Now this move does evade the first difficulty, but it has problems of its own. For instead of assuming that that which is greater than everything exists in reality, he now assumes that *something exists in reality*, and from that concludes that if that which is greater than everything exists in the understanding alone, then it is less than this something that exists in reality, and thus not greater than everything.

This assumption, that something exists in reality, is no small matter. Its importance, and the effect it may have on the argument, can be felt in different ways, all of which are connected with the contingency of the claim itself.[20] Here I am not just interested that one can doubt this claim; for my aim is not to criticize Gaunilo's argument, but to show that it is not Anselm's. Rather, I believe a crucial difference can be displayed between the arguments in question even if we accept the above matter of fact assumption as true. Given that Gaunilo's version requires a factual premise, that is, given that an argument which employs "that which is greater than everything" requires the contingent presupposition that something exists in reality, we may now question the suitability of this phrase for proving, in a rigorously logical manner, "the real existence of the thing spoken of."[21]   For if Gaunilo's argument contains a factual premise, then it loses a certain character which I think is importantly present in Anselm's argument. This, I hope, can be brought out by noticing that in Gaunilo's version he omits what I have taken to be a central premise. We are now in a position to see why he must do this and how this distinguishes his argument from Anselm's. The premise that Gaunilo neglects is the one that reads:

> *Et certe id quo maius cogitari nequit non potest esse in solo intellectu.*

> And surely that than which a greater cannot be thought cannot exist in the understanding alone.

It is the *"non potest"* ("cannot") that I have been stressing: Anselm is claiming in this line, and claims to be able to show with his *reductio*, that something than which nothing greater can be thought *cannot* exist in the understanding alone. Gaunilo must leave this out because, so far as I can see, he is not able to show this with his argument. For given the contingency of his assumption, he could never show that that which is greater than everything cannot exist in the understanding alone. As a matter of fact, it *can*. That is to say, there is nothing in itself inconsistent about claiming that that which is greater than everything exists in the understanding alone. For in a world in which, as a matter of fact, all other things failed to exist in reality, that which is greater than everything can itself fail to exist.

The real point, as Anselm saw, is the difference in the phrases that are employed. "That which is greater than everything," if it may be put this way, depends for what it is upon that "everything" than which it is greater. If that "everything" does not exist in reality, then there is no reason why that which is greater than everything should. But the minute the argument becomes dependent upon what facts obtain, it loses its rigor. "Something than which nothing greater can be thought" is, on the other hand, not dependent for what it is upon what is, in fact, the case. For while Gaunilo must assume that something exists in reality which is greater than what exists in the understanding alone, we have seen that Anselm need not claim that there actually exists something which is greater than what exists in the understanding alone, but only that something greater *can be thought*. Anselm neither does assume nor need assume that anything is, in fact, the case for his argument to work. This is why when he comes to the premise in which existence in reality is mentioned, it is guarded with a careful "can be thought." It reads:

> . . . if it exists in the understanding alone even, it *can be thought* to exist in reality also, which is greater.

In this form, the premise simply will not work for Gaunilo. For as Anselm himself suggests, it is *not* at all evident that because something greater *can be thought* than that which is greater than everything, that that which is greater than everything fails to be that which is greater than everything.[22]

Gaunilo, then, deviates from Anselm's argument not just at this critical point but, we might say, from the very beginning in so far as he substitutes another phrase for the key phrase. Such a change has essential bearing upon the argument and the result, as I have tried to show and as Anselm himself claimed in his fifth reply, is that Gaunilo offers a version of the argument which altogether misses the subtlety of Anselm's own reasoning. The matter is one, if it may be said again, of the strange relationship of form to content with respect to the way in which the key phrase affords a method of arguing. A change in the content of this phrase necessitates a change in the form of the argument. And this change in the form of the argument, which we have just now inspected, turns out to mean nothing less than an entirely different argument.[23] Anselm was clear about this and so it is no wonder he would have disavowed Gaunilo's characterization of his reasoning as "nowhere in all that I have said . . ."

I am not so much concerned with Gaunilo's mistake *per se*, as I am that we do not make it. Gaunilo misses the point of Anselm's argument, that is, he never sees its subtlety. The key to the argument lies in the power of the phrase: "something than which nothing greater can be thought." To change that phrase is to change the argument itself. More importantly, not to be equal to this phrase, that is, not to appreciate the delicate moves Anselm can make by means of it, is to fall short of the argument. It is this which we do again and again, each time we present Anselm's argument in hackneyed one-liners like:

The Greatest Being exists in reality, for otherwise it wouldn't be the Greatest Being.

or some such "argument" which leads one to believe that its originator was a simpleton, rather than an accomplished, indeed, innovative logician. The real mistake comes when we attempt to paraphrase, substitute, and finally package the entire argument in a single convenient line. Such simplified versions always turn out to be little better than simple-minded.

Gaunilo betrays Anselm's argument when he changes the key phrase. What follows from this is not only the need to change the strategy of the argument, but a transformation of premises along the way, all resulting in a change in the very conclusion which follows from that argument. Warned by his mistake, let us now attempt to adhere as closely as possible to Anselm's own argument to see if we can return, both to his reasoning and to its conclusion, some of its original force and rigor.

In the last section, we have interrupted our discussion of the development of II on order to inspect a certain misunderstanding of that chapter. To recall the argument as I have presented it, let us consider the reasoning of II in the following summary form:

1) God is something than which nothing greater can be thought.
2) "Something than which nothing greater can be thought" is understood.
3) Whatever is understood exists in the understanding.
4) Whatever exists in the understanding either exists in the understanding alone or exists both in the understanding and in reality.
5) That than which a greater cannot be thought cannot exist in the understanding alone:
   a) Whatever exists in the understanding alone, can be thought to exist in reality also, which is greater.
   b) Consequently, whatever exists in the understanding alone is that than which a greater can be thought.

    c) If then that than which a greater cannot be thought exists in the understanding alone, the very same that than which a greater cannot be thought is that than which a greater can be thought; but this is impossible.

    d) Thus 5 is shown.

6) Therefore there is absolutely no doubt that something than which a greater cannot be thought exists both in the understanding and in reality.

Notice that on my account the *reductio* argument is employed to show *only* premise 5 and is not meant to be an argument sufficient unto itself for showing the existence both in the understanding and in reality of that than which a greater cannot be thought. Rather, this conclusion (i.e. 6) follows from a direct demonstration which employs a *reductio* along the way in order to show one of its premises (i.e. 5). The logic of this direct demonstration that shows 6 is given in the following steps:

A) From 2 and 3 we conclude that something than which nothing greater can be thought exists in the understanding.

B) It follows then from A, together with 4, that something than which nothing greater can be thought either exists in the understanding alone or exists both in the understanding and in reality.

C) Now 5 shows that something than which nothing greater can be thought cannot exist in the understanding alone. This, together with the disjunct of B allows us to conclude that without doubt, something than which nothing greater can be thought exists both in the understanding and in reality.

We must now attempt to get some sense of what this conclusion is, that is, exactly what it says. I think the more we come to understand it, appreciating the full force of the premises from which it follows, the more we will come to see that Anselm's argument tends to be sold short; not only in the simplified misrepresentation that I have called the classical misunderstanding, but in most accounts of the reasoning of II.

According to Anselm's own argument, the conclusion runs:

Existit ergo procul dubio aliquid quo maius cogitari non valet, et in intellectu et in re.

Therefore, there is absolutely no doubt that something than which a greater cannot be thought exists both in the understanding and in reality.

While I think it is fair to say that, ordinarily, the conclusion is assumed to be: something than which a greater cannot be thought exists; or even, if more precisely because of a recognition of the distinctions made in Chapter II, one might carefully say: something than which a greater cannot be thought exists both in the understanding and in reality. In either of these two ways of putting the conclusion, there is something neglected. The decisive omission is the *"procul dubio."* This is translated by Charlesworth as "absolutely no doubt." But what does it mean to say that a conclusion is "without doubt"?

I would like to begin by suggesting that the neglect of the *"procul dubio"* in the conclusion of II corresponds to another oversight that I have taken pains to bring into prominence: the failure to appreciate the force of the *"non potest"* in premise 5. We have seen that Gaunilo does not take this *"cannot"* seriously, and that his version of the argument, unlike Anselm's own, is not even designed to sustain the conclusion that: something than which a greater cannot be thought *cannot* exist in the understanding alone. For his version rests on a factual assumption, notably, the assumption that something exists in reality. Anselm's *reductio*, on the other hand, does not appeal to any matters of fact. He does not assume, nor need he assume that something exists in reality which is greater than what exists in the understanding alone. Rather he assumes (or shows) that something greater *can be thought* than what exists in the understanding alone, and this latter claim holds independently of what is or is not the case. So far as I can see, there is no point in the development of Anselm's reasoning at which he relies upon factual premises.[24]

The "without doubt" of the conclusion of II, therefore, directly corresponds to the "cannot" of premise 5. For the central strategy of the reasoning in II is to show something than which nothing greater can be thought *cannot* exist in the understanding alone after it has already been conceded that it either exists in the understanding alone or exists both in the understanding and in reality. If the one alternative is impossible, then the other is without doubt; that is, *there is no possible alternative*. And so Anselm concludes that it is wholly without doubt that something than which a greater cannot be thought exists both in the understanding and in reality. The conclusion, then, is apodictic. It does not follow from something not being the case, as it would were it claimed that something than which a greater can be thought, as a matter of fact, does not exist in the understanding alone. Nor does it follow from something being the case, as in the classical misunderstanding, which assumes that something, in fact, exists in reality. Rather, it strictly follows from something that has been shown to be impossible.

This *"procul dubio,"* then, is no idle matter, and no mere ornament to the conclusion of II. Instead, it reveals a great deal about the nature of the reasoning as well as the force of the conclusion that is intended to follow from that reasoning. This conclusion tells us that in so far as it is impossible that something than which nothing greater can be thought exists in the understanding alone, there can be no doubt that it exists both in the understanding and in reality. And this is important. For precisely what makes one feel uneasy about allowing such a conclusion is that we assume it could be otherwise; we tend to say that logic cannot decide such matters because they could always be otherwise, in fact. However, precisely what Anselm is trying to claim is that, in fact, it could not be otherwise. Something than which nothing greater can be thought does not just happen not to exist in the understanding alone, it *cannot*. And since we have already admitted that it either exists in the understanding alone, or both in the understanding and in reality, Anselm concludes, without doubt, something than which a greater cannot be thought exists both in the understanding and in reality.

With this we have adequately completed the development of the reasoning of II. We have not, however, arrived at what Anselm claimed to set out to show, and about this we should be clear. For according to Anselm's expressed intention in the title of II, he was to offer us an argument that claimed to show: *Quod vere sit deus.* From the reasoning of II, however, Anselm sees fit only to conclude that: *Existit ergo procul dubio aliquid quo maius cogitari non valet, et in intellectu et in re.*[25] In other words, Anselm has not claimed to have concluded anything about "God" but rather about "something than which a greater cannot be thought" nor has he attempted to conclude that anything (be it God or something than which nothing greater can be thought) "truly exists" but only that it "exists both in the understanding and in reality." To find further mention of both *deus* and *vere esse*, we shall have to turn to III.

Chapter 2

Proslogion III

We are now prepared to enter *Proslogion* III. And our preparation should prove vital, for I shall not be treating III as a separate argument, independent of II. The basis on which I allow this understanding of the relation of II to III can be disclosed only after we have gotten the reasoning of III before us. At that point I shall discuss not only this interpretation of the connection between II and III, but will consider as well some other accounts that have been given. Needless to say, how one construes the connection between these two chapters is crucial to their understanding. Without going into detail here, let me just say that precisely in as much as I refuse to recognize in III a separate proof for the existence of God, that is, one independent of the reasoning that has already been developed in II, much of the burden that is today put on III, by those who find an independent proof there, will be removed. Without the demand to justify such a proof in III, we should be able to move swiftly through an argument which Anselm himself presents with no little brevity.

It should be clear from what has already been said that I believe too much of the wrong sort of attention has been given to III in recent years. The attempt to find a separate proof there has not only placed a demand on the chapter which Anselm never appears to have suited it for, but it has also distracted us from seeing the proper place of the chapter in Anselm's argument. It has, however, done something else, and this is my second reason for hoping to give no more attention to this chapter than Anselm did: locating Chapter III as the crucial chapter has destroyed the balance between II, III and IV. This lack of balance is not something that recent interpreters alone are to be blamed for. In fact, they themselves complain that for too long all the weight has been given to II, and not enough to III. And yet neither those who find the entire argument in II nor those who find the crucial argument in III seem to give any attention to IV. Now, this is as ironic as it can be, for it is in IV that the Fool is answered, that is, it is *in IV* that *the conclusions to be gleaned from II and III are drawn by Anselm himself*. Despite the fact that this chapter should be at the center of the argument, it hardly seems to be discussed at all. It is my hope, then, that after our development of III, and its relation to II, we will be in a position to deal with IV in proper detail.

The reasoning of III is, to say the least, succinct. There is no development or clarification such as we encountered in II. As a matter of fact, the entire argument occurs in two lines. The first runs:

> *Nam potest cogitari esse aliquid, quod non possit cogitari non esse; quod maius est quam quod non esse cogitari potest.*

> For something can be thought to exist that cannot be thought not to exist, and this is greater than that which can be thought not to exist.

Precisely because the argument is so compressed, we will have some unraveling to do. There is a good deal going on in this deceptively straightforward sentence, and one can easily be misled.

Let's begin by attempting to sort out the content of the sentence. There seem to be three phrases, all of the same apparent form, which dominate the line. These phrases are:

   i) can be thought to exist
  ii) cannot be thought not to exist
 iii) can be thought not to exist.

All three are similar, and differ only through the inclusion of "not." I would like to suggest that, as in II, these phrases are related to each other in a special sort of way that is not at all easy to make out. Let us take a hint from II. If we recall our discussion of the three phrases: "exists in the understanding," "exists in the understanding alone," and "exists both in the understanding and in reality," we will remember that it was important to realize that these three phrases were not all, so to speak, of the same order. Rather, given that something existed in the understanding, two options remained open: either it existed in the understanding alone, or existed both in the understanding and in reality.

I believe the three phrases that occur in III are related in much the same way. In other words, given that something can be thought to exist, we can then pose the question of whether it can be thought not to exist, or cannot be thought not to exist. Now i and iii may appear to be in contradiction to one another, but precisely what we must come to see, if we are to understand what Anselm is getting at, is that they are not. For it is not a contradiction to say that something can be thought *to exist* and can be thought *not to exist*. We are *not* here saying that something *can* be thought to exist and *cannot* be thought to exist. This latter case would be a contradiction, for it is not intelligible that something both can and cannot be thought to exist. Anselm is saying something quite different, however. He is saying that even once we admit that something can be thought to exist, we may still pose the question of whether it can be thought not to exist.

At this point, it may seem as if we are confronting a maze of "can" and "cannot" and of "exist" and "not exist."[26] This should be taken as a warning of how difficult and precise the conceptual machinery of III is. The mastery of these distinctions is a requirement for understanding the reasoning that follows, and it is clear that if we fail to conquer the terminology we run the risk of misconstruing entirely what is going on here. So it is important that we make no little effort in attempting to get it straight.

We must get clear then about the meaning and relation of the three phrases at issue. I have already begun by suggesting that the recognition of i is essential to the significance of *both* ii and iii. To put this otherwise, the "something can be thought to exist" of:

> . . . something can be thought to exist that cannot be thought not to exist, and this is greater than that which can be thought not to exist . . .

ranges over not only the "cannot be thought not to exist" but the "can be thought not to exist" as well. As I am reading this line then, it runs: something can be thought to exist that cannot be thought not to exist, and this is greater than something that can be thought to exist that can be thought not to exist. And it is my claim that unless we realize that the "can be thought to exist" precisely refers to (and is in no way in contradiction to) what "can be thought not to exist" we lose the significance of this latter phrase, as well as the contrast that Anselm is trying to make out. We shall return to this point in a moment, but let us now turn to inspecting the phrases one at a time.

The first phrase that we must have a look at begins the sentence: something can be thought to exist. Its introduction tells us that whatever is to be discussed subsequently in III is something that can be thought to exist. A possible confusion is, however, hidden here; one we have already encountered in our discussion of the "can be thought" (*"potest cogitari"*) of the line in II that reads:

> . . . if it exists in the understanding alone even, it can be thought to exist in reality also . . .

We saw there that the "can be thought" was part of the form of the argument, such that this phrase says; . . . if it exists in the understanding alone, then one can think: something that exists in reality also. So in III, when Anselm says that "something can be thought to exist that cannot be thought not to exist," what he is saying is that one can think: something that exists that cannot be thought not to exist. Or in the case of the claim that something can be thought to exist that can be thought not to exist, he is saying; one can think: something that exists that can be thought not to exist. The "can be thought" of the phrase "can be thought to exist" is part of the form of the argument, and not part of the content of the phrase. This is only true in the case of the one phrase. In the other two phrases the "can be thought" figures into the actual content.

It may appear arbitrary to say that in the one case, and in the one case alone, the "can be thought" is *not* part of its content, while in the other two cases it is. In a sense, this should be very obvious, *if* we understand what the contrast is that Anselm is trying to make out here, and *if* we appreciate that his argument must be in a form appropriate to something than which nothing greater *can be thought*. The phrase which introduces the contrast will determine the form of the argument. This phrase is the first: can be thought to exist. The other two phrases, however, will involve the content of the contrast that is being made out in III. This is why they will occur again in the argument itself, while the "can be thought to exist" will not.

With this "something can be thought to exist", then, a twofold purpose is being accomplished. First of all, Anselm is limiting the scope of the "something" ("*aliquid*") for the argument of III. Secondly, at the same time, he is keeping the reasoning in line with his key phrase. For the sake of the form of the argument, we are at all points interested in what *can be thought*. On the other hand, as a result of the reasoning of II, he has every right to limit what is being spoken of in III to what "exists both in the understanding and in reality." Indeed, the very fact that he uses "exist" without qualification, that is, does not speak of "exists in reality" or "exists in the understanding alone" indicates that he feels it is evident that we are talking about what exists both in the understanding and in reality. So these two intentions: to limit the scope of the "*aliquid*" in III to what exists (both in the understanding and in reality), and to maintain the contrast to follow in a form appropriate to something than which nothing greater can be thought, determine the first phrase: "can be thought to exist."

This is only the starting point; We now need to come to understand the other two phrases that go along with the first, and present the contrast which is the focal point of Chapter III. And this is why it is important to realize that the scope of the "*aliquid*" is limited in III to what exists, for in so doing Anselm is able to give a force to the other two expressions that would otherwise be lacking.

If we recall the sentence that we are in the process of analyzing, then it should be plain that Anselm presents us with two alternative cases, both of which he wants to say can be thought: something that exists that cannot be thought not to exist, and something that exists that can be thought not to exist. Let's begin with the latter case. It is of the utmost importance to realize that when we speak of something that can be thought not to exist, we are speaking of something that exists. For, in a sense the claim that something *can* be thought not to exist retains a significant force only if we are thinking about something that exists.[27] That this is what Anselm has in mind, that is, that he is talking about what does in fact exist when he speaks of what "can be thought not to exist," is made sufficiently clear in a reply:

> ... *quidquid est praeter id quo maius cogitari nequit, etiam cum scitur esse, posse non esse cogitari.*

> ... whatever exists, save that than which a greater cannot be thought, can be thought of as not existing *even when we know that it does exist.*[28]

I have added the emphasis to show that what "can be thought not to exist" is not what fails to exist, but precisely what exists, is known to exist, and yet, for all that, can still be thought not to exist.

This brings us to our other case: something that exists that cannot be thought not to exist. Anselm wants to claim that this can be thought and, of course, that it is greater than what exists and yet can be thought not to exist. One may be rather mystified as to exactly what Anselm has in mind when he speaks of something that cannot be thought not to exist. In a reply, however, he gives us a very definite answer to this question:

> *Illud vero solum non potest cogitati non esse, in quo nec initium nec finem nec partium coniunctionem, et quod non nisi semper et ubique totum ulla invenit cogitatio.*

> Only that in which there is neither beginning nor end nor conjunction of parts, and that thought does not discern save as a whole in every place and at every time, cannot be thought not to exist.[29]

Apparently, when Anselm speaks of something that cannot be thought not to exist, a cluster of characteristics are called to mind: beginningless being, utterly simple, that is everywhere and always whole (*semper et ubique totem*).[30] That such a being was without beginning, of course, would not mean that it failed to exist (as it would mean with any other being) but rather that there was never any point at which it began, nor therefore a time before it existed which could be thought. And, as simple, this beginningless being would also be endless; presuming that what is simple cannot be destroyed. Furthermore, it could not exist at some particular place and some particular time rather than another (lest it could be thought not to exist), but would instead exist wholly, everywhere and always. Such a being then (if it is proper to speak of *a* being here) would enjoy the unique benefit of being that which alone cannot be thought not to exist.

I said earlier that *if* we understood the contrast that is being made out in III, and further understood the need to keep to a certain form for the sake of the argument, we would understand the difference and the relationship among the three phrases: can be thought to exist, cannot be thought not to exist, and can be thought not to exist. Let us see if we have succeeded in understanding this, in any measure.

The actual contrast that is being made out here is between something that cannot be thought not to exist, and something that can be thought not to exist. The reasoning that follows centers around this distinction. For these phrases to have their proper force, however, we must realize that what we are talking about is in all cases something that exists (both in the understanding and in reality); in other words, we must realize that in III the scope of the "*aliquid*" is limited to what exists. For in speaking of what can be thought not to exist, we must be completely clear that we are talking about something that exists, is known to exist, and *nevertheless* can be thought not to exist. Contrasted with this, of course, is what exists, is known to exist, and yet, cannot be thought not to exist.

Given that this is the contrast being made out, it must be put very carefully. What we are told is that something can be thought to exist that cannot be thought not to exist, that is, one can think: something that exists and cannot be thought not to exist. Contrasted with this is the claim that one can think: something that exists and can be thought not to exist. This is then coupled with the claim that the former is greater than the latter. And again, this is why the "can be thought" of the first phrase (can be thought to exist) appropriates the distinction to follow to the form the argument requires. For what this line claims is that one can think: something that exists that cannot be thought not to exist, and in so far as this is greater, the whole point that Anselm wants to make is that *something greater can be thought* than something that exists that can be thought not to exist.

I doubt that I have been able to make out the full force of what Anselm is claiming in III. It is far more weighty than the question of whether something than which nothing greater can be thought exists or not. That question has been settled. And only if we accept that something has been shown to exist in reality, will the full force of what it means to inquire whether it can be thought not to exist come through, and so the true significance of this strange claim that something cannot be thought not to exist. It is very difficult to get a grasp on the distinction being drawn here, so we shall return to it later in this chapter.

What Anselm understands to follow from the line we have just discussed is given without delay:

> *Quare si id quo maius nequit cogitari, potest cogitari non esse: id ipsum quo maius cogitari nequit, non est id quo maius cogitari nequit; quod convenire non potest.*

> Hence, if that than which a greater cannot be thought can be thought not to exist, then that than which a greater cannot be thought is not the same as that than which a greater cannot be thought, which is absurd.

We should already be familiar with this sort of move from II: in so far as we recognize that something greater can be thought than what can be thought not to exist, if that than which a greater cannot be thought can be thought not to exist, the very same that than which a greater cannot be thought is not that than which a greater cannot be thought. Notice once again that the "*id ipsum*" is employed at the point where the notion of identity is being stressed. The very same being both is and is not that than which a greater cannot be thought; that is, if we assume that something than which a greater cannot be thought can be thought not to exist. But that something is not itself cannot possibly be concluded.

It is clear how this claim to identity is used to generate the contradiction for the *reductio*:

> . . . if that than which a greater cannot be thought can be thought not to exist . . .

is the assumption of the negation of what is to be shown by the *reductio*. We want to show that something than which a greater cannot be thought cannot be thought not to exist, and so for the sake of the argument, we assume that it can be thought not to exist. Almost as quickly as we assume this, we see a contradiction following:

> ... then that than which a greater cannot be thought is not the same as that than which a greater cannot be thought ...

a claim which is clearly absurd. Something cannot both be the same and not the same as itself and, as we shall see, this is especially true in the case of something than which nothing greater can be thought.

Now this must all seem terribly simple, for everyone knows full-well the form of a *reductio*. But there is something odd here, if we look at what is concluded from it. For what one would expect to be concluded from a *reductio* is the negation of what is assumed. This is the form of the *reductio*: in order to show something, assume it is not the case, and derive a contradiction. But it is clear then that what is shown by a *reductio* is precisely that which the assumption is the negation of. In this case, the assumption was:

> ... if that than which a greater cannot be thought can be thought not to exist ...

In other words, the assumption is that it can be thought not to exist. If this leads to contradiction, then what has been shown is that it cannot be thought not to exist, and this should be rightly concluded from the argument. But look at what Anselm concludes:

> *Sic ergo vere est aliquid quo maius cogitari non potest, ut nec cogitari possit non esse.*

> Something than which a greater cannot be thought exists so truly then, that it cannot be even thought not to exist.

And this would be a somewhat different conclusion than one would expect to follow from the *reductio* alone. As a matter of fact, this conclusion is exactly like the first line of the chapter (a line we have not discussed) except that this line includes the "something than which a greater cannot be thought." It seems clear that the conclusion we are given above is the one Anselm wants to argue for, as he announces it in the first line of III, and it seems equally clear that he thinks he has shwon this when he claims it to be his conclusion, immediately after the *reductio*. And yet, it does not seem to follow. So far as I can see, only the last part of the conclusion (that it cannot be thought not to exist) follows from the *reductio* of III. But where does the "exists so truly" come in?

I believe that I have already suggested an answer to this all-important question, and now we must go into it in some detail. First we must be clear on the question. Anselm begins Chapter III claiming that he intends to show:

Quod utique sic vere est, ut nec cogitari possit non esse.

and concludes the reasoning of III convinced he has shown that:

Something than which a greater cannot be thought exists so truly that it cannot be even thought not to exist.

And yet, all that seems to follow from the *reductio* of III is that something than which a greater cannot be thought cannot be thought not to exist. It is not at all clear at what point the "so truly exists" ("*sic vere est*") enters the reasoning of III. Is Anselm claiming that because something cannot be thought not to exist that it follows that it exists (so truly)? Is this "so truly exists" a sort of corollary that follows from the *reductio*, but which is simply never demonstrated explicitly? Or is this "so truly exists" intended to follow from the *reductio* of III in any way at all?

If we look closely at the text itself, it should supply us with answers to these and similar questions. Let us take note of a few facts about the use of the phrase "so truly exists." The first chapter in which this phrase occurs is III, and as a matter of fact, it occurs in the very first sentence of III. This is, indeed, the first time *in* a chapter that the phrase occurs, but it does occur before this, as a chapter heading. Strangely enough, the chapter heading in which it occurs is not III, which is entitled: *Quod non possit cogitari non esse*, but rather that of II: *Quod vere sit deus*, or: That God truly exists. One cannot help taking this mention of the use of "truly exists" in the text as a hint to its origin. It begins Chapter III, but seems to make reference back to the title of II. And, of course, I have already suggested above that it is crucial for a proper understanding of III that we realize that what is spoken of there is already accepted as existing (both in the understanding and in reality). It might seem, then, that the "truly exists" has already been shown in II and is simply being conjoined with the "cannot be thought not to exist" that is shown in III to arrive at the complex conclusion that something "truly exists" and "cannot be thought not to exist."

I am afriad that it would be a serious mistake to settle the matter so easily. For if Anselm had shown that something "truly exists" in II and now was simply going on to show that it "cannot be thought not to exist" in III, it is odd that he does not tell us this in II. I do not mean that he fails to tell us this explicitly, but rather it is odd that the "truly exists" is never mentioned in II at all. Instead, in II, Anselm uses the phrase "exists both in the understanding and in reality" throughout. On top of that, the "truly exists" does come up again in III. For even though *vere esse* occurs in its chapter heading, the conclusion of II is that something than which nothing greater can be thought exists both in the understanding and in reality, while each time that the *vere est* occurs in III, it occurs with the phrase *non possit cogitari non esse;* that is, it only occurs with a phrase that itself is not brought up until III.

What becomes eminently clear from all this, it seems to me, is that there is a great deal of confusion surrounding the relation and connection of the two chapters in question, namely, II and III. Much has been speculated about this, and even more assumed. What we now need is a consideration of the alternatives with an attentive eye fixed upon the text. We must attempt to ascertain what the argument itself suggests the relationship of II and III to be, and further ask how well the available accounts of that relationship measure up against a standard as rigorous as the text itself.

There are a number of basic accounts of the relation of II to III that are either explicitly argued for, or simply implied by interpreters of Anselm. We cannot hope to go into all the varied accounts in detail

in what follows. So I shall, first of all, limit myself to those interpretations which accept that there is a philosophical proof for the
existence of God going on somewhere in the *Proslogion*. Of the interpreters whose accounts are in some way or other connected with the
question of the existence of God, I shall further limit myself to those
that seem to make a fundamental decision as to the relationship of
these two chapters. And although each of the views I will discuss is
held by someone, I intend them also as *general* positions, which should
give the reader a *general* sense of the alternative accounts that could be
offered.

The first account which needs to be mentioned is one that has long
been the traditional way of interpreting Anselm. Actually, it is impro-
per to think of this as an *account* of the relation of II to III for, in this
traditional interpretation, any account of that relation is wholly impli-
cit or, more precsiely put, assumed. This interpretation presupposes
that the entire argument for the existence of God is contained in
Chapter II. There is no mention of III made at all; as if Anselm never
wrote it, or at best, as if it had nothing to do with his argument for the
existence of God. On this view, Anselm's argument begins and ends in
II. Now, we shall see later that there is a more sophisticated account
that shares this view, but with an awareness and an explicit interpretation and understanding of the place of III in the argument. At this level
however, that is, at the level of the traditional interpretation, III is
simply never mentioned at all and the argument is assumed to be in II
and nowhere else.

The naive assumption which fails even to pose the question of III
would itself seem to be enough to deem this interpretation inadequate,
particularly in more recent years when so much concern has arisen as
to exactly what Anselm's argument is. Simply to assume that it is in II
and ignore III will not do. But it is not only for this reason that it is
inadequate. There is a textual reason, one to which I have already
alluded, that reveals its error; a fact that I shall be returning to again
and again in attempting to measure any account against the standard of
the text itself.

I believe that the reason many have been led to think the argument
for the existence of God is in II has been the title of that chapter:
Quod vere sit deus, that God truly exists. It has been assumed that this

is what II attempts to show. If we look at II, however, we see that it claims to have shown nothing of the kind. Instead, what it concludes is that: something than which a greater cannot be thought exists both in the understanding and in reality. Not only is "God" not mentioned here; it is also evident that the "truly exists" is lacking, unless of course, we further assume that "exists both in the understanding and in reality" is equivalent to "truly exists." Such an assumption becomes unlikely when we realize that the "truly exists" does occur again, in III, and furthermore always occurs in conjunction with "cannot be thought not to exist." And although we cannot, at this point, go into the connection between these two phrases, it is clear that the "truly exists" which is announced as the title of II does come up again, only not in II.

This claim that I am making, that the "truly exists" of the title of II is in some way connected with III, is not an idle speculation, but would have been apparent to anyone who had read and understood IV, as we shall see when we get there. And chapter IV is without any doubt related to II in that it is meant to be an answer to the Fool, who claims (in II) that God does not exist. If we look at IV, we shall see that the phrase "exists both in the understanding and in reality" never occurs there, which strongly indicates that Anselm did not think that what was shown in II was sufficient to answer the Fool. There are other factors about IV which could be discussed, but we don't want to get ahead of ourselves. The only reason I mention it is because the traditional interpretation assumes II to be an adequate answer to the Fool, indeed, assumes it to be Anselm's entire answer. But as IV makes evident, this is simply not the case.

The inadequacies of this traditional interpretation have been apparent since attention was drawn to Chapter III by Norman Malcolm, in his article "Anselm's Ontological Arguments."[31] Once one is aware that Chapter III is in some way connected with a proof for the existence of God, it will no longer do to assume that Anselm's argument is in II alone, and nowhere else. Now, Malcolm is not the only one who has supposed the tradition to be amiss. Charles Hartshorne has also offered an alternative interpretation, and along the same lines as Malcolm.[32] Hartshorne, however, is a bit more vehement in his chiding of the tradition for not having read Anselm carefully enough, and he implies that the lack of scholarship in this matter borders on criminal neglect. In some sense then, this recent reinterpretation of Anselm sees itself as moving against the traditional account we have sketched above.

In Malcolm's and Hartshorne's view, it is III and not II that is the crucial chapter. They believe that Anselm gave (although they would not claim he realized it) two different arguments for the existence of God: one in II and another in III. The argument of II they find unredeemable, and agree with the tradition as to its interpretation and the reasons for its inadequacy:

> Anselm's ontological proof of *Proslogion* 2 is fallacious because it rests on the false doctrine that existence is a perfection (and therefore that "existence" is a "real predicate").[33]

One could hardly find a more traditional argument against II, and I think it is important to realize that what this indicates is that neither Hartshorne (who rejects it for the same reason) nor Malcolm makes any serious attempt to rethink II. Rather, they discover a "second argument" in III, and latch onto it. Indeed, after a very brief account of II, Malcolm turns to a rather lengthy discussion of III:

> I take up now the consideration of the second ontological proof, which Anselm presents in the very next chapter of the Proslogion. (There is no evidence that he thought of himself as offering two different proofs.)[34]

It is interesting that Malcolm puts this last sentence parenthetically. As we shall see, not only is there no evidence that Anselm thought of himself as giving two separate arguments; there is evidence to the contrary. Yet, following this remark, Malcolm continues unimpeded in his discussion, and after quoting the *reductio* portion of III, together with its conclusion (and we would do well to remember that it is this very conclusion that forced us to pose the question of the relation of II to III), he finally concludes:

> Previously I rejected *existence* as a perfection. Anselm is maintaining in the remarks last quoted (from Chapter III), not that existence

is a perfection, but that *the logical impossibility of nonexistence* is a perfection. In other words, *necessary existence* is a perfection. His first ontological proof uses the principle that a thing is greater if it exists than if it does not exist. His second proof employs the different principle that a thing is greater if it necessarily exists than if it does not necessarily exist.[35]

Malcolm goes on to defend this latter principle. It should be clear from this what sort of account of the relation of the chapters in question is implied: there are two separate and independent arguments given in Chapters II and III of the *Proslogion*. One of these is claimed to be fallacious, while the other is applauded as a shrewd bit of reasoning.

Although it must be admitted that we have much to thank Malcolm (and Hartshorne) for in terms of forcing us out of the naive assumption of the traditional view, I believe that it is nonetheless fair to say that even this more recent account never systematically poses the question of the relation of II to III. For while it is claimed that there are two separate and independent arguments operating in II and III (and therefore assumed that each chapter can stand alone), and while it is further admitted that Anselm would not have seen himself as giving two separate arguments, the question is never raised whether the text, as it stands, can bear such division. Neither Malcolm nor Hartshorne attempts to show that it is possible to sever II from III without sacrifice. And one would only assume this must be shown, if it is admitted that the original author never intended the separation.

In this sense, the Malcolm/Hartshorne interpretation is more traditional than they might think. First off, it is odd that if one felt he had been led astray by a traditional interpretation that ignores III, he would assume that this same tradition had not led him astray in its interpretation of II. But there is no attempt made to reinterpret II in light of the recognition of III. Instead, both Malcolm and Hartshorne accept the traditional understanding of II as well as, and this is most crucial, the traditional assumption that II is a complete and separate argument. We have already seen, in our attack on the traditional account, that there is good reason to suspect even from the title of II that II and III are intimately connected, for what is claimed in the title of II is not shown until III. This in itself should make us wonder if II is capable of standing on its own as a complete and separate argument for the existence of God.

There is, however, a more important issue to be considered. What is supposed to lead us to believe that III is a complete and separate argument? If II precedes III, can we afford to assume that the latter does not presuppose the former, and that in rejecting II (as Malcolm and Hartshorne do) we have not rejected certain premises that are required for III? I have already tried to show that Anselm enters III assuming we have already accepted the argument of II, that is, that we have already accepted that what we are talking about (something than which nothing greater can be thought) has been shown to exist both in the understanding and in reality. But if we reject II, we must reject this also, and enter III not knowing whether or not what we are talking about exists. Of course, those who find a separate proof for the existence of God in III would agree; we do not enter III already knowing that something than which nothing greater can be thought exists both in the understanding and in reality, for this is what (or part of what) is claimed to be shown by III. The question then becomes: Can Chapter III, as it stands, support the added burden which this account would place upon it?

My interest here is not to deal with the soundness of the argument that Malcolm offers as the second proof, but only to judge the accuracy of his account as an account of Anselm, that is, of the original text as it stands. In his argument, Malcolm claims that Chapter III deals specifically with what he calls "the logical impossibility of nonexistence." This is Malcolm's understanding of Anselm's phrase "cannot be thought not to exist." Apparently he takes the "cannot be thought" to be a reference to what we today call logical impossibility. We shall return to this point in a moment; but there is something else we must take note of first. In the above quoted passage, Malcolm identifies "the logical impossibility of nonexistence" with what he calls "necessary existence." Presumably then, Malcolm would treat as equivalent all three of these phrases. To say that something necessarily exists is to say that it cannot be thought not to exist, which is just another way of saying that its nonexistence is logically impossible.

Not only is it obvious that Anselm never uses the phrase "necessarily exists" in III, it is also true that he would not have identified "necessar-

ily exists" without "cannot be thought not to exist."[36]   Rather, what
necessarily exists is what "cannot not exist," not what cannot be
thought not to exist, and this is made clear in a reply in which Anselm
actually does argue that something than which a greater cannot be
thought necessarily exists.[37]   Furthermore, certain replies clearly indicate that Anselm separated "cannot not exist" from "cannot be
thought not to exist" and so would have separated "necessarily exists"
from "cannot be thought not to exist."[38]

A natural way to respond might be to admit this but go on to claim
that Anselm and Malcolm simply differ in their use of "necessarily
exists."   What Malcolm means by "necessarily exists" then is what
Anselm means by "cannot be thought not to exist" (that is, the logical
impossibility of nonexistence) while the category "cannot not exist"
may simply be put to the side.   Nevertheless, the question certainly
remains to be asked: Does Anselm mean by "cannot be thought not to
exist" the same as Malcolm means by "the logical impossibility of non-
existence"?

An answer to this question has already been given in an extremely
brief, though nonetheless decisive, article that appeared after the publication of Malcolm's account of Anselm's arguments. In that article,[39]
G. B. Mathews shows that if the *"possit cogitari"* ("can be thought") of
Anselm's phrase *"non possit cogitari non esse"* ("cannot be thought not
to exist") were to be understood in terms of what is today called "logical possibility" there would be some unfortunate implications. Notably, in Chapter XV of the *Proslogion* in which Anselm argues that
something than which a greater cannot be thought is *"maius quam
cogitari possit"* ("greater than what can be thought") taking the *"possit
cogitari"* as a reference to logical possibility would result in Anselm
claiming that God is greater than is logically possible; that is, that God
is logically impossible.   Hardly a view that Anselm means to be
embracing.

My interest in this is not just to suggest that Malcolm has Anselm
wrong on a number of important points, but to raise the question of
why Malcolm performs the transformations of Anselm's own phrases
which he does.   Why does Malcolm employ the phrase "the logical
impossibility of nonexistence"?   Why doesn't he retain Anselm's own
phrase "cannot be thought not to exist"?   I can only offer one answer
to this: it would seem extremely odd for someone to argue that if

something cannot be *thought* not to exist, it follows directly that it exists. Such an inference manifestly confounds categories. This is made even more striking when we realize that there is no need for Anselm, if he wants to show that something (necessarily) exists, to interpose the word "thought" into the reasoning of III. Instead, he could have argued that it cannot not exist without complicating matters by the inclusion of "thought" unless, of course there is a specific purpose in this, independent of the proof that something exists, or even that it necessarily exists. But to show that something cannot be *thought* not to exist would scarcely seem to entail as a direct consequence that the something in question existed. Malcolm must alter Anselm's own words in order to present an argument that might pass itself off as a proof for the existence of something. This is not to endorse Malcolm's inference from "logically impossible not to exist" to "exists" as sound, but it is to say that at least his way of putting it does not wear confusion on its face.

Malcolm's "second ontological proof," then, turns out to be as different from the reasoning of III as it is claimed to be from II. For there is simply no point in attempting to offer the argument that shows that something than which a greater cannot be thought cannot be thought not to exist as a separate proof for the existence of anything. On the contrary, Anselm had already shown that something than which a greater cannot be thought exists both in the understanding and in reality *before* attempting to show that it cannot be thought not to exist. Whatever other significance Malcolm's ontological arguments may have, it is clear that his treatment is wholly inadequate as an interpretation of Anselm.

There is a third account of the relation between II and III, offered by D. P. Henry, which is a more sophisticated twist on the traditional interpretation. In Henry's view, the entire argument for the existence of God is located in II, and while he is quite aware of the presence and importance of III, he does not see it connected with II in so far as III is claimed not be a consideration of the existence of God, but of the nature of God. Once God has been shown to exist (*et in intellectu et in re*) in II, on this view, Anselm then proceeds to consider the nature of that being he has just proven to exist. Consequently, III is not taken to have anything to do with the question of the existence of this being.

Precisely in so far as this interpretation is like the first, it falls to the same criticism. It is convenient that what I take to be its weakest point Henry claims as its basis. It is worth quoting him here. He begins an article on "Proslogion Chapter III" as follows:

> The headings of chapters 2 and 3 of St. Anselm's *Proslogion* are respectively: *Quod vere sit deus* and *Quod non possit cogitari non esse*. They would therefore appear to be concerned with diverse questions.[40]

This might be a compelling point, if only those chapters did answer these diverse questions *in themselves*. The fact is, however, that the titles of both chapters and their contents are not perfectly in line.[41] The aim declared in the title of II is not arrived at until III; for not only is "God" not brought up in II, the "truly exists" isn't either. Given that what is to be shown is that God truly exists, it is clear *if we look at the text* that this is not concluded until III; while the title of III is itself not entirely in accord with the conclusion announced in that chapter.

The difficulty with Henry is that although he sees clearly the difference between II and III, he does not see their connection. This is a difficulty common to all three of the interpretations we have so far encountered. If there is any one assumption that they share, it is that Chapters II and III contain separate and independent arguments. But if I read Anselm right, we can think no such thing. Any number of issues brought up in the text, including his own discussion of the answer to the fool in IV, would do more than enough to suggest that II and III belong together. This does not mean that there may not be different things going on in each; that is, it does not mean that they are merely repetitions of one another, but neither does it mean that they are separate arguments.

And this brings us to a fourth interpretation; so far as I know, one of the most recent. In this account, put forth by Richard La Croix, there is only one argument (the *unum argumentum* Anselm promises in the Preface) for the existence of God in the *Proslogion*, and that one argument is the *Proslogion* itself. No chapter or series of chapters can be singled out from the rest of the work as the proof for the existence of God. In this way, every chapter belongs together with every other chapter as part of one argument. Chapters II and III then, also belong together.

Now, in a sense, it is unfair to claim that II and III belong together in the same way that other chapters do. For what La Croix is claiming here is that II and III together show a series of existential deductions about the being than which a greater cannot be thought. What he says is that:

> In *Proslogion* II Anselm deduces claim (c) that the being than-which-a-greater-cannot-be-thought exists ... In *Proslogion* III Anselm deduces claim (d), that the being than-which-a-greater-cannot-be-thought cannot be thought not to exist ... In the chapters subsequent to *Proslogion* IV Anselm similarly deduces a series of claims which taken together imply the claim (a′), that the being than-which-a-greater-cannot-be-thought bears the properties traditionally attributed to God.

This means that:

> ... *Proslogion* II and III do not separately contain logically complete arguments for the existence of God but rather ... the two chapters taken together ... form the basis for a series of deductions about the existence of a being minimally characterized as that-than-which-a-greater-cannot-be-thought ... Anselm does not purport in either of these Chapters to establish that God exists where the proposition "God exists" is taken to mean "the being bearing the properties traditionally attributed to God exists." It was shown that in Anselm's actual procedure it is the entire *Proslogion* that is intended to establish the claim that God exists ....[42]

On this view, once it has been established that a being than which a greater cannot be thought exists in reality, and cannot be thought not to exist, the task remains in the subsequent chapters of the *Proslogion* to establish that this being (than which a greater cannot be thought) is God, that is, that all the attributes that we would normally attribute to God can be attributed to this being than which a greater cannot be thought. So Chapters II and III go together and serve to show a series of deductions about a being "minimally characterized" as a being than which a greater cannot be thought, and the rest of the work serves to demonstrate that this "minimally characterized" being, which has been shown to exist and cannot be thought not to exist, is God.

Once again, the real issue is whether or not this interpretation of Anselm can hold its own when judged against the text. If La Croix is correct, then at the end of III, nothing has yet been shown about God, but only about something than which nothing greater can be thought. However, Anselm does bring God up again in III. For at about the middle of that chapter, immediately after the conclusion is stated, God returns:

> *Sic ergo vere est aliquid quo maius cogitari non potest, ut nec cogitari possit non esse. Et hoc es tu, domine deus noster. Sic ergo vere est, domine deus meus, ut nec cogitari possis non esse.*

Something than which a greater cannot be thought exists so truly then, that it cannot be even thought not to exist. And You, Lord our God, are this being. You exist so truly, then my Lord my God, that You cannot even be thought not to exist.

It certainly appears as if Anselm is prepared to identify something than which a greater cannot be thought with God at the level of III. La Croix takes notice that Anselm does this, but attempts to dismiss it as an expression of religious enthusiasm, indeed, a premature expression, that as yet has no ground in argument.[43] Even assuming that this were true, it would not tell us why Anselm sees fit to answer the Fool in IV. Notice that in La Croix's characterization of the proper place of the various chapters of the *Proslogion*, he never tells us how IV fits in. He says that II and III deal with the existence of this being, and that the chapters *subsequent* to IV deal with the traditional attributes of God, but he says nothing at all about IV itself. And with good reason. For in IV, a Fool is answered who does not claim that something than which a greater cannot be thought does not exist, but who clearly and unequivocally is presented as claiming that God does not exist. Indeed, the discussion of IV is centered around "God." Anselm is not hesitant to use this word in the way in which he is not only hesitant, but never uses it in the argument of II, and only finally in III. Can IV also be written off as premature?

Assuming that one does not attempt to go back to the beginning of II and claim that an equivalence between "something than which nothing greater can be thought" and "God" obtains throughout, and I think La Croix is right in suggesting that we need more than this,[44] the question remains whether anything that has been argued in II or III would justify Anselm's claim in III that God is something than which nothing greater can be thought, that is, that: ". . . You, Lord our God, are this being." Why does Anselm say this, on what basis and why at this point and not before?

I believe that if we take the above question, and begin with the last part first, we may find our answer. Let us look again at what Anselm has to say at precisely this point in III, and what it is that has been shown:

> And You, Lord our God, are this being. You exist so truly, then my Lord my God, that You cannot even be thought not to exist.

It is here that we first come upon something that so truly exists that it cannot be thought not to exist. It is clear that at this point, for the first time in the argument, that is, only after the reasoning of III (which on my reading is itself dependent upon the reasoning of II) have we come to see that something than which nothing greater can be thought cannot be thought not to exist. Now, later on in the same chapter (III) we are told, speaking of God that:

> *Et quidem quidquid est aliud praeter te solum, potest cogitari non esse.*
>
> In fact, everything else there is, except You alone, can be thought of as not existing.

In other words, it is clear to Anselm that God *alone* so truly exists that He cannot be thought not to exist. In a reply (IV) this "*non possit cogitari non esse*" ("cannot be thought not to exist") is referred to as "the distinguishing characteristic" ("*proprium*") of God.[45]

It is little wonder then that Anselm felt justified in bringing God up in III, if what distinguishes Him from all else is precisely that He exists so truly that He cannot be thought not to exist, since as soon as it is established that something than which a greater cannot be thought exists so truly that it cannot be thought not to exist, it is evident that something than which nothing greater can be thought is God. Where La Croix makes his mistake is to assume that Anselm will not be justified in calling anything "God" until he has shown it to possess *every*

attribute that God is thought to have. On the contrary, once we have
come upon the *distinctive* character of God, we are justified in calling
whatever it is that has this character by the name "God."[46]

I believe La Croix is incorrect in claiming that the entire *Proslogion*
is to be taken as Anselm's argument for the existence of God. More
importantly, his claim concerning the unity of the entire text not only
obscures the issue of the *specific* relatedness of II and III, but also fails
to appreciate the completeness and fullness of those chapters as they
stand. This is not to deny that it might be of assistance in understanding the argument of II and III to study the entire work, but is to claim
that there are logical grounds for separating off certain chapters as an
argument for the existence of God, independent of others and adequate
unto themselves. *Which* chapters one separates off, however, is the
crucial matter.

With this we come to the most difficult part of the analysis of alternative accounts of the relation of II to III, that is, the demand to suggest one that seems to be in line with the text. It has been rather easy
to show what is wrong with the four basic interpretations sketched
above; but the reason it is so easy to attack accounts of this relation is
the difficulty involved in outlining an interpretation that lines up with
the text at all points. The easiest way to do this is to let the argument
itself suggest an interpretation, and this can best be made out by appealing to the text.

We have already stressed that the proclaimed title of II and the purpose of the argument is to show: "*Quod vere sit deus*," while the actual conclusion of II states: "*Existit ergo procul dubio aliquid quo
maius cogitari non valet, et in intellectu et in re*." In II then we neither
come to the "*vere esse*," nor to "*deus*," but only to the "*existit in
intellectu et in re*" of "*aliquid quo maius cogitari non valet*." Now, this
would not be as odd as it is if it were not for the fact that both the
"*vere esse*" and "*deus*" come up again in III. And what's more, both
come up only after a number of steps in III have been taken; only after
the reasoning of III has been completed. Furthermore, the "*vere esse*"
of III always occurs in conjunction with the title of III: "*non possit
cogitari non esse*." What are we to take this to mean?

I believe this strongly suggests that when Anselm says that God truly
exists he means that God so exists that He cannot be thought not to
exist. This is why "*vere esse*" is never mentioned in II, and when it is

finally concluded in III, what we are told is that He truly exists in such a way that He cannot be thought not to exist. Strictly understood, then, when Anselm speaks of the *"vere esse"* of *"deus"* in the title of II, he is referring to a specific way of existing.[47] To show that something than which nothing greater can be thought truly exists (in this strict sense) would require showing that it exists both in the understanding and in reality, but it would also require something more; that is, existing both in the understanding and in reality would be a necessary, but not a sufficient condition for its truly existing. Such a view, of course, is highly suggestive of the relation of II to III. For II would not be a separate and complete argument to show that God truly exists, although it would have its place as the first stage of such an argument, and would be sufficient to show that something than which nothing greater can be thought exists both in the understanding and in reality. In order to show that this something than which a greater cannot be thought truly exists, one would have to go on to show that it exists both in the understanding and in reality in such a way that it cannot be thought not to exist.

Clearly, this would allow us to explain the conclusion following the *reductio* of III that first led us to the question of the relation of these two chapters. For the line which claims that:

> *Sic ergo vere est aliquid quo maius cogitari non potest, ut nec cogitari possit non esse.*

> Something than which a greater cannot be thought so truly exists then, that it cannot be even thought not to exist.

would no longer be understood as the conclusion of the *reductio* of III alone, but rather would follow from the reasoning of II and III together. This means *not* that we have simply conjoined the conclusion of II with the conclusion of III, but that this conclusion follows from a single argument which employs Chapter II as its first stage. For it is not claimed that God truly exists in II, but only that something than which nothing greater can be thought exists both in the understanding and in reality. Having shown that this something which exists both in the understanding and in reality cannot be thought not to exist would then allow us to conclude that it truly exists.

Not only, then, would II and III serve different purposes, but at the same time, they would be a single argument. For while II is insufficient to show that something than which a greater cannot be thought truly exists, it claims to be sufficient to show that it exists both in the understanding and in reality. And while III is insufficient by itself to show that anything exists, when coupled with II it belongs to an argument which shows that something than which nothing greater can be thought truly exists, that is, so exists that it cannot be thought not to exist. This way of taking Anselm not only explains why God's existence is not concluded in II, but also allows us to comprehend the origin of the conclusion of III; a conclusion which could not be deduced from the *reductio* of III alone. In short, II and III belong together as a single argument, and it is only this argument which shows that God truly exists.

It would appear that at the center of my account of the relation of II to III lies this understanding of the "*vere esse.*" For if "*vere esse*" has nothing essentially to do with "*non possit cogitari non esse,*" then there is no reason to believe that by "*vere esse*" Anselm means anything more than "*existit et in intellectu et in re.*" If this were the case, there would be no need of III to show that God truly exists, but this (or at least that something than which nothing greater can be thought truly exists) would have been shown in II. There then would be no reason to think that II and III go together. For it is critical to my interpretation that the claimed and announced purpose of the argument in the title of II not be completed in II. It may well be, so one might be tempted to argue, nothing more than a coincidence that Anselm never uses the words "*vere esse*" in II. What needs to be shown is that there is some important conceptual connection between the "*vere esse*" and the "*non possit cogitari non esse,*" that is, that Anselm really does think that God truly exists means: God exists in such a way that He cannot be thought not to exist; not simply an appeal to the "fact" that he fails to use the words "*vere esse.*"

The place to begin looking for a response to this objection is a passage from *Proslogion* XXII in which "cannot be thought not to exist" is directly connected to the way of existing appropriate to God alone. That chapter begins:

Tu solus ergo, domine, es quod es, et tu es qui es. Nam quod aliud est in toto et aliud in partibus, et in quo aliquid est mutabile, non

omnino es quod es. Et quod incepit a non esse et potest cogitari non
esse, et nisi per aliud subsistat redit in non esse; et quod habet fuisse
quod iam non est, et futurum esse quod nondum est: id non est
propie et absolute. Tu vero es quod es, quia quidquid aliquando aut
aliquo modo est, hoc toto et semper es. Et tu es qui proprie et
simpliciter es, quia nec habes fuisse aut futurum esse, sed tantum
praesens esse, nec potest cogitari aliquando non esse.

You alone then, Lord, are what You are and You are who You are.
For what is one thing as a whole and another as to its parts, and has
in it something mutable, is not altogether what it is. And what
began to exist from non-existence, and can be thought not to exist,
and returns to non-existence unless it subsists through some other;
and what has had a past existence but does not now exist, and a
future existence but does not yet exist—such a thing does not exist
in a strict and absolute sense. But You are what You are, for whatever You are at any time or in any way this You are wholly and for-
ever. And You are the being that exists in a proper and absolute
sense because You have neither past nor future existence but only
present existence; nor can You be thought not to exist at any
time.[48]

Contrasted with God here is what is mutable and thus not wholly what
it is. In so far as anything had its beginning from non-existence, and if
not held to stand by another turns back to non-existence, it can be
thought not to exist. And what had a past which no longer exists and a
future that does not yet exist does not exist properly, that is, absolutely. Here *"absolute"* must be taken in a twofold sense: firstly, what
does not exist absolutely does not exist *fully* or *completely*. It has a
past and a future, and is yet to be completed. But in a second sense,
what does not exist absolutely does not *purely* exist; its existence is
blended with non-existence. And in so far as it has arisen from non-
existence, and will return to non-existence unless supported by another,
it does not exist *"proprie,"* that is, its existence is not strictly its own.
   God, on the other hand, exists properly and simply.[49] For God
there is no "has been" or "not yet," such that there is something that
God is not now but will be or has been. Rather, God is wholly and always what He is. Having only present existence, that is, always existing
fully, there is no time at which God can be thought not to exist. For

that which is without part or alteration, without a past in which it rose from non-existence or the future threat of returning to non-existence, cannot be thought not to exist. Indeed, this very description reflects the one given in the replies of an utterly simply being, without beginning or end, which is everywhere and always whole.[50] All these characters Anselm seems to treat as captured by the expression "*non possit cogitari non esse*." For that something is without beginning and end is analogous to the claim that it is without past and future, and both matters concern the possibility of it being thought not to exist, since for any being that has a beginning, a time can be thought before which it did not exist (or if it has an end a time after which), and were it not everywhere and always whole (were it at some particular place at some particular time) it would be possible to think a place and time at which it was not, and so it could be thought not to exist. And, certainly it must be without part or alteration; that is, it must be both simple and immutable, for if it were not simple thought could decompose it into parts, and so think it not to exist. And, finally, if something is utterly simple in this way (not only without parts, but always existing fully), then it is clearly immutable; all of which is to stress that a good many characteristics are entailed by the claim that something cannot be thought not to exist and that by appealing to these characteristics Anselm is able repeatedly to assert that God exists in a way in which He alone can.[51] This is expressed in different language. The passage from *Proslogion* XXII tells us that God alone exists simply and properly; but this is directly connected up with another way of putting it: God alone exists in such a way that He cannot be thought not to exist. In fact, this latter character of His existence is (in Reply IV) referred to as "the distinguishing character" ("*proprium*") of God. This in itself should indicate that there is a sense of "exist" in which it is true to say that God alone exists.

An even stronger case is made for this claim in an earlier work. The force of what Anselm intends to show is made plain in the title of the XXVIIIth chapter of the *Monologion*:

Quod idem spiritus simpliciter sit, et creata illi comparata non sint.

That this Spirit exists simply, and created things compared to it do not exist.

The chapter itself begins as follows:

> *Videtur ergo consequi ex praecedentibus quod iste spiritus, qui sic*
> *suo quodam mirabiliter singulari et singulariter mirabili modo est,*
> *quadam ratione solus sit, alia vero quaecumque videntur esse, huic*
> *collata non sint.*

Therefore, it seems to be consequent from the preceding that this
Spirit which exists in so wonderfully singular and singularly wonderful a way of its own, in a certain manner alone exists; indeed, any
other things whatever that seem to exist, compared to It do not
exist.[52]

This is a very strong way to put the point: God alone exists. God
exists in a way of His own, and in this sense of "exist," nothing else
exists; even stronger, compared to this way of existing, all other things
do not exist. The claim that there is a way of existing which applies to
God alone is emphasized in the play on "*mirabilis*" and "*singularis*," for
both words can mean singular, strange, extraordinary, but the
"*singulariter*" can also mean exceedingly. So to say of something that
it is "*singulariter mirabili*" not only underscores its extraordinary singularity ("*mirabiliter singulari*") but stresses that such singularity is
exceedingly extraordinary.

If we were to follow the development of this chapter throughout, I
think it is safe to say we would find that it is strikingly similar to
Proslogion XXII, for Anselm goes on in this chapter from the
Monologion to characterize the existence appropriate to God as
"*simpliciter et absolute et perfecte*." It suffices to say that Chapter
XXII of the *Proslogion* is something like a highly condensed version of
Monologion XXVIII, and what is significant in this is that in both
places Anselm is striving to bring out the same crucial point: In a certain sense, God alone exists.

In the view that I am suggesting this whole family of characteristics
which Anselm employs to give expression to this way in which God
(alone) exists can be summed up under the single rubric "*vere esse*."
To say that God truly exists, then, would mean that God exists immutably, simply, properly, absolutely, that is to say, in the way that distinguishes God from everything else: in such a way that He cannot be

thought not to exist. This *"vere esse"* would then just be a condensed way of saying all of this, and would mean that God properly exists, that God truly exists, in a way in which nothing else does or can.

As a matter of fact, in Gerberon's Standard Edition of Anselm's works there is a passage in which this is made exceptionally clear. Unfortunately, the more recent Critical Edition of F. S. Schmitt does not include this passage.[53] The first Meditation in the Gerberon text is so enlightening on this matter, however, that we simply must have a look at it. The portion that concerns us reads:

> *Ego, ait, sum qui sum. Et pulchre. Ipse enim vere solus est cuius immutabile est esse. Ille itaque, cuius esse tam excellens, tam singulariter est, ut solum vere est, in cuius comparatione omne esse nihil est . . .*[54]

> I, he said, am who I am. And this is beautifully said. For that alone truly exists whose existence is immutable. Accordingly, He whose existence is so excellent, so singular, alone truly exists in comparison to which all other existence is nothing . . .

Whoever the author, one cannot help being struck by the similarity of expression between this and the other passages both from the *Proslogion* and *Monologion*. To begin with, the meditation is inspired by the same saying that is being alluded to at the opening of *Proslogion* XXII, where it is claimed that *"tu es qui es."* As in XXII, we are told that this applies to God alone (*"solus"*) and further this is immediately grounded in the notion of immutability, while in the *Proslogion* precisely what is being claimed is that *"mutabile"* must be rejected from what *"es quod es."* Furthermore, like the passage from *Monologion* XXVIII, singularity (*"singulariter"*) is again stressed; only here it is characterized in terms of *"vere esse,"* and we are told that in this way of existing, God alone truly exists (*"solum vere est"*). Finally, this passage ends on the same note that XXVIII is designed to bring out: that compared to the wonderfully singular and singularly wonderful way in which God exists, all other beings do not exist; or, as it is put so simply here: in so far as God alone truly exists, compared to Him, all else is nothing.

The author of this short passage, then, sees fit to draw together the whole cluster of characteristics of God's existence; that it is singular, simple, absolute, perfect, immutable, etc., all under the title *"vere esse."* And as has been adequately demonstrated by Stolz, the employment of *"vere esse"* to designate the sort of existence appropriate to God alone is not unique to this author, but has a history that dates back to Augustine.[55]

Given this understanding of the *"vere esse"* it should be evident that there is a direct and significant connection between "truly exists" and "cannot be thought not to exist." As we have seen, both of these phrases are employed to characterize the existence of God; that God truly exists in a way that nothing else does or can; He truly exists in that He cannot be thought not to exist. A clear connection between these categories can be seen across the passages we have inspected above. The passage from *Proslogion* XXII identifies this "cannot be thought not to exist" in terms of simple, absolute, immutable existence. In *Monologion* XXVIII this absolute, simple, perfect existence is claimed to be so singular that, in some sense, God alone exists, while other things compared to Him do not. Finally, in the meditation just offered this singular, immutable existence, compared to which all else is nothing, which we have seen can be characterized in terms of "cannot be thought not to exist" in so far as this is the distinguishing feature (*"proprium"*) of God, is all gathered under the *"vere esse"* and it is claimed, perfectly in line with the other two passages, that God alone truly exists. On this basis, it is far from coincidence that Anselm never uses *"vere esse"* until III and that it is always given in conjunction with the "cannot be thought not to exist." For precisely what it means to say that God truly exists is to say that God exists in a way in which nothing else can, indeed, in such a way that, by comparison, all else is nothing. God so exists that He cannot be thought not to exist and, in this sense, He alone truly exists.

I believe it has now been sufficiently demonstrated that the objection that there is only a nominal or coincidental relationship between the *"vere esse"* and the *"non possit cogitari non esse"* is without ground. At the same time, I think the very considerations which demonstrate this have also shown that nothing in particular hinges upon the use of the *"vere"* in the title of II. Its employment was simply

taken as a hint which might lead us to developing the issues we now
have.   For our claim about the need for III in order to complete
Anselm's task is not at all nominal (that a word isn't used in II, to wit:
"vere") but essential: II is conceptually inseparable from III.   For
Anselm fully appreciated the unique singularity of God's existence, and
does not claim his argument to have brought us to this until the
reductio of III has been concluded.   For to show that *God* exists demands that we show Him to exist *in the way in which He* exists.   And
given what we have seen concerning the special use of "exists" which
must be employed with regard to God, it can now be argued, and I
think immediately seen, that even were the title of II: That God exists;
that is, even were the 'truly' omitted from that title, I could still make
out my claim about the necessary relatedness of II and III.   For there
can be no doubt that Anselm consistently holds that God exists in a
way wholly unlike anything else, and it must be exactly this existence
which is shown if one is to show the existence of God.

I have, for convenience and nothing more, appealed to the matter of
the *vere esse* to bring this point home.   But even without it, we should
be able to employ the above discussion in conjunction with the important (and now understandable) textual fact that "God" is not mentioned in the conclusion of II, but only returns to the argument after
the reasoning of III and, therefore, after the conclusion of the single
argument which spans II and III to the effect that: something than
which nothing greater can be thought truly exists in such a way that it
cannot be thought not to exist.   This not only provides a reasonable
basis for identifying something than which nothing greater can be
thought with God (in that this *sic esse ut non possit cogitari non esse* is
the distinguishing character [*propium*] of God), but only at this point
have we arrived at that existence one can properly claim to be God's.

In some sense, then, the question of the *"vere esse"* and the question
of the *"deus"* which I employed in measuring the other accounts of the
relation of II to III are separate issues.   For even if there were no *"vere"*
in the title of II, one could nevertheless raise the question of the *"deus"*
and why it occurs in the title of II but not in the chapter's conclusion.
At the same time, in another sense, it is clear that these two issues go
together, for it is precisely in so far as Anselm is interested in showing
the existence of God (which must mean, from what we now know, that

singular existence appropriate to God) that he aims to show that something truly exists, that is, so exists that it cannot be thought not to exist. Were Anselm to attempt to show anything less than this he would simply have defaulted on his promise to demonstrate the existence of God. He must show that God truly exists if he is to succeed. Manifestly, this is not shown in II, but is shown (or at least claimed to have been shown) only by the single argument that spans the reasoning of both II and III.

Elaborating the essential connection between *vere esse* and *non possit cogitari non esse* in the argument serves to do quite a bit more than answer a possible objection, and more even than the important job of helping to clarify in some detail the significance of those expressions. For our discussion has also divulged the specific relatedness of II to III, and their necessary connection. We have said that II is conceptually inseparable from III, and now can make explicit how this is. For it may even be misleading to think of II and III as separate steps in a single argument, since III moves beyond the conclusion of II only in so far as it moves within it. To show the existence of God involves bringing into view an existence which is radically singular. II provides the incomplete claim that something than which nothing greater can be thought exists, and as such grounds the undertaking which focuses upon this very existence in determining whether or not it is of the radically singular sort characterized by the *non possit cogitari non esse*. The project, to show the existence of God, is only carried through to completion, that is to say, only receives conclusive treatment by pursuing the matter in III. But III is bound to the conclusion of II for it serves to bring that conclusion to adequate precision; or, as we have put it, moves beyond it only in so far as it moves within it. Nevertheless, II cannot stand alone since it does not, by itself, claim to show the existence *of God*; that is, the existence which is God's own and God's alone.

Understanding the specific relatedness of II to III not only allows us to identify the argument, but should assist us in finding our way to its strategy. For III does not, on its own, attempt to show that anything exists in reality. Instead, it presupposes that this *aliquid quo nihil maius cogitari possit* exists (from II) and then aims to show that it enjoys that singularity of existence the *non possit cogitari non esse* expresses. The conclusion stated in III, then, is not simply a conjoining of the conclusion of II and the conclusion of the reasoning of III, but is the result, and can only be the result, of a single argument which is begun in II and completed in III. Only this single argument can sufficiently clarify the existence appropriate to something than which nothing greater can be thought and, in so doing, justify us in concluding that it is, indeed, God (that exists).

To be sure, then, II and III serve different purposes, and yet a conceptual necessity binds them together into a single argument. II provides the fundamental but inadequate and inconclusive claim that something than which nothing greater can be thought exists both in the understanding and in reality, while III is required to complete the expressed project by pursuing the existence of this something than which a greater cannot be thought in order to certify that it enjoys the existence appropriate to God.

The problem of the relation of II to III has been settled. What it means to say that God truly exists is that God so exists that He cannot be thought not to exist. It is this which Anselm must demonstrate before he has shown that God exists, and it is this which is claimed as the conclusion of III. This conclusion, however, does not follow from the reasoning of II or from the reasoning of III alone. On this basis I differ with the accounts of the tradition which has misunderstood Anselm, with Malcolm who has attempted to re-interpret him, and with D. P. Henry who adds some scholarly reputability to the traditional view. At the same time, I believe that there is a basis in the text for claiming that the single argument of II and III attempts to demonstrate the existence of God, and on this point I find myself at odds with La Croix's account. On my view, there is a single argument which is begun in II and completed in III and which, if sound, would be sufficient to show the existence of God.

If I am right about the relationship of II to III, then nothing can be more misleading than the claim that a separate and independent argument for the existence of God is going on in III. This is especially misleading in that it distracts us from the real import of that chapter. We shall, then, have to inquire into its actual significance. Even more importantly, another issue has been raised in our discussion of the basic accounts of the relation of II and III which will unfold itself throughout the remainder of this work. At this point, we may state it as follows: in so far as each interpreter of Anselm we considered found a different argument, they each, at the same time, found him to be urging different claims.   Henry read the argument's conclusion as claiming that God exists, Malcolm as that God necessarily exists, etc. So it still remains to be determined what force the conclusion of Anselm's argument commands given the account I have offered of the relation between II and III. We shall proceed by turning to the former matter and in so doing will, of course, touch upon the latter. Elaborating the full force of the argument, however, is a difficult matter and will, in effect, remain unsettled until the conclusion of this book. Nonetheless, we should keep it in mind as we turn to the question of the significance of III.

Certainly the central matter for thought in III is the distinction between something that exists in such a way that it cannot be thought not to exist, and something that exists in such a way that it can be thought not to exist. We have already seen that for these two phrases to have their full force, we must in both cases be speaking of something that exists. So when we speak of something that can be thought not to exist, we are speaking of something that exists, is known to exist, and nevertheless can be thought not to exist. It has already been indicated that of all the beings that exist, thought has the power to think any of them not to exist, except one. This being alone cannot be thought not to exist, that is, truly exists. This very distinction then, between what can be thought not to exist and what cannot be thought not to exist, is sufficient to mark a difference between all the beings that exist, and the one that truly exists.   Indeed, this is not *a* difference, but *the* difference.

It is not surprising, then, that in the second half of III, after the conclusion of the argument of II and III has been stated, God returns and the creator/creature distinction is invoked:

Et hoc es tu, domine deus noster. Sic ergo vere es, domine deus meus, ut nec cogitari possis non esse. Et merito. Si enim aliqua mens posset cogitare aliquid melius te, ascenderet creatura super creatorem, et iudicaret de creatore; quod valde est absurdum. Et quidem quidquid est aliud praeter te solum, potest cogitari non esse.

And You, Lord our God, are this being. You exist so truly, then Lord my God, that You cannot even be thought not to exist. And this is as it should be, for if some intelligence could think of something better than You, the creature would be above its creator and would judge its creator—and that is completely absurd. In fact, everything else there is, except You alone, can be thought of as not existing.

Most evidently, Anselm is saying that it is fitting that God is something than which nothing greater can be thought, for if any mind could think something greater (or "better": "*melius*"), then in so thinking that something is greater, that creature would be passing judgment on its creator. Of course, in Anselm's view, it is exactly the reverse that is true: the creator judges the creature. Understanding these lines in this way, however, does not tell us why the mention of absurdity of creature judging creator is placed between the repeated claim that the creator cannot be thought not to exist. For when Anselm says: "And this is as it should be" ("*Et merito.*") he must also be referring to the last thing he has said: ". . . that You cannot even be thought not to exist." And after having told us that it is exceedingly absurd that a creature should judge the creator, he repeats that "everything else, except You alone, can be thought of as not existing." I believe this suggests that far more than stressing here only that it is fitting a mind should not be able to think anything greater than God, Anselm is at the same time saying it is fitting that a creature cannot think the creator not to exist. And *not* because a creature depends upon its creator, but because a creature is not properly in a position to pass any judgment on its creator. In so far as God cannot be thought not to exist, thought is not free to decree any alternative opinion. In other cases, thought must make some judgment as to whether or not the matter it is thinking is to be thought as existing or not. In this case however, *thought is determined by the matter it is thinking.*[56] For in the process of attempting to think "something than which nothing greater can be thought," thought discovers that in order to grasp the matter (i.e. something than which nothing greater can be thought) it is determined to think something which so exists that it cannot be thought not to exist. This means that it must be thought uniquely, that is, in full recognition of the difference between what can be thought not to exist (creature) and what alone cannot be thought not to exist (creator).

It is to this point of bringing us to an awareness of this difference that III is directed. For it is meant to show that:

> *Et quidem quidquid est aliud praeter te solum, potest cogitari non esse. Solus igitur verissime omnium, et ideo maxime omnium habes esse: quia quidquid aliud est non sic vere, et idcirco minus habet esse.*

In fact, whatever else there is, except You alone, can be thought not to exist. You alone, then, most truly of all, and therefore to the highest degree of all, possess existence: because anything else exists not so truly, and therefore possesses existence to a lesser degree.

This is a very sticky passage which is easily misinterpreted thanks to its allusion to that strange (and often confusing) medieval doctrine of degrees of reality. To begin with, although it is clear this claim, that things do not so truly exist, follows from the claim that God possesses existence most truly of all, we must be aware that Anselm is *not* here saying that God exists more truly than other things. The contrast is not between existing more truly and existing less truly. In the first place this is because Anselm does not speak of existing less truly, but of "possessing existence to a lesser degree" (*"minus habet esse"*). Moreover, what Anselm claims is not that God possesses existence more truly than all other things, but rather that God possesses existence *most* truly of all; not that God possesses existence to a higher degree, but that God possesses existence to the highest degree (or maximally). To claim, then, that God most truly of all possesses existence is not to make a claim to comparison, but to claim for God a right to distinction. In this sense, it may be a serious confusion to think that saying that all other things "exist not so truly" means nothing other than that they exist less truly. This latter claim is never made by Anselm. What he says is that all other things possess existence to a lesser degree *because* they exist *"non sic vere."*

The crucial issue that we must not lose sight of is stated in the very first line: anything else (indeed, everything else) except God alone, can be thought not to exist. It is from this claim that the second sentence follows. This latter sentence is replete with inferential language. These inferences all follow from the recognition of the general claim of the first line. In so far as everything except God can be thought not to exist, which, of course is to claim that God cannot be thought not to exist, it follows that God alone most truly possesses existence, which is to say that God possesses existence to the highest degree. But what does this follow from? Clearly, that God alone cannot be thought not to exist. It is crucial to recognize here the direction in which these inferences move. It is because God alone cannot be thought not to exist that we can conclude that He most truly and to the highest degree of all possesses existence.

At this point, a very interesting suggestion is made by Anselm and this we must give careful attention to. He says that: because anything else does not exist so truly, it therefore possesses existence to a lesser degree. If what possesses existence to the highest degree is identified with what cannot be thought not to exist, then surely what possesses existence to a lesser degree must be identified with what can be thought not to exist. This view is verified if we juxtapose this line with the first line given. Their forms are so similar that it is clear they are intended to go together:

   . . . quidquid est aliud . . . potest cogitari non esse.

   . . . quidquid aliud est non sic vere . . .

What we are told across these two lines is that anything else there is can be thought not to exist, and in so far as it can be thought not to exist, exists not so truly. Put otherwise, if what so exists that it cannot be thought not to exist truly exists, then what so exists that it can be thought not to exist, in so far as it exists in this way, does not truly exist. Notice what follows from this. Since everything else exists not so truly, it follows that it exists to a lesser degree. How are we to take this? It is certainly correct to say that if something does not truly exist to such a degree then it exists to a lesser degree. For if something does not exist to such a degree as something else, it certainly does exist to a lesser degree. This, however, is not even informative, let alone significant. What Anselm is saying here is that in so far as everything else does not truly exist in this way (in the way in which God alone exists, that is, cannot be thought not to exist) it follows that it exists to a lesser degree. This would tell us that in so far as anything can be thought not to exist, it exists to a lesser degree than God, Who alone cannot be thought not to exist, and therefore, in terms of degrees, exists to the highest. For what we are being informed of at the end of III, in this line that speaks of degrees of existence, is that God *both* exists to a specific degree *and* exists in a specific way. Indeed, these two belong together: God exists to such a degree that he exists in a certain way.

In this passage from III, however, the emphasis is rather the opposite of that just stated; for we have seen Anselm argue that *because* God exists in a certain manner, He exists to the highest degree. This is why it is important to notice the direction of the inferences. Anselm does not claim that because God exists to the highest degree, He exists in a unique manner. Quite the opposite. What he claims is that in so far as God exists in such a way that He cannot be thought not to exist, it follows that He exists to the highest degree.

It is evident that this passage at the end of III is a reference to the little understood doctrine of degrees of existence; less evident, however, is its intention to display the singular existence which is God's in terms of that doctrine. To appreciate this we must be clear on exactly what it means to say that something "*verissime et maxime habes esse.*" And our understanding of this must involve something more than the correct, but uninformative observation that it means something exists to the highest degree. A clue is being offered by Anselm when he connects "most truly of all and therefore to the highest degree of all possesses existence" with the claim that God alone "cannot be thought not to exist." This tells us that to say something exists to the highest degree is *not* to say that it exists in a higher degree than other things, but to emphasize that it exists in a way wholly unlike anything else; that it exists simply and absolutely, immutably and in a singularly wonderful manner of its own, in short, that it alone cannot be thought not to exist.

The allusion, then, to the doctrine of degrees of existence, as well as the appeal to the creator/creature distinction immediately following the conclusion of the argument, are both aimed at bringing into prominence a matter which, if understood, may make it possible for us to feel more fully the force of the claim *Proslogion* III is designed to show, and so the actual weight of the conclusion of Anselm's argument which is stated there. For throughout this chapter, what has been at issue is the

difference between what so exists that it can be thought not to exist
and what so exists that it cannot be thought not to exist; that is, the
difference between the existence of God and the existence of everything else. This enormous difference has been compressed into a single
distinction in III. We have, however, in the process of coming to grips
with this distinction found ourselves developing it in some detail with
the help of Anselm's own deliberations in this chapter as well as in
other texts. And I believe, if thoughtfully consulted, these deliberations all bear directly on a certain unique character of the God-question
which may not have struck us as yet.

My interpretation appears to put Anselm in the position of needing
to be able to show more than one might ordinarily think. For it may
seem enough of a task to demonstrate that something exists without, at
the same time, needing to show that it so exists that it cannot be
thought not to exist. I have argued that Anselm must show exactly this
before he can claim to have demonstrated that God exists, and, of
course, my account aims to show that the text itself declares this not to
be more than is necessary, but exactly what is appropriate. In this
event, it would not be the case that I have made things too hard for
Anselm, but that we ordinarily make things too easy on ourselves. For
given what Anselm claims in III, it becomes evident that he deals with
the question of the existence of God as altogether unlike the question
of whether or not one more being should be included in the realm of
existing creatures. Indeed, the claim that God alone truly exists serves
to radically exclude Him from this realm. In so doing, Anselm signals
his commitment to the position that raising the question of the existence of God begins a more strenuous ordeal than is ordinarily understood to be involved in showing that something exists in reality. On his
account, asserting the existence of God entails the paling of what we
ordinarily call real; as if against the measure of what so exists that it
cannot be thought not to exist, all that can be thought not to exist
recedes into irreality. For if God exists in a way wholly unlike everything else; in such a way that even those things which we ordinarily
affirm as existing, when compared to Him, vanish into nothing; then,
presumably an adequate treatment of the question of God's existence
would require the application of thought's power to annul (*potest
cogitari non esse*) the entire realm of existing creatures in order to clear
the way for an appropriate answer.

Properly speaking, then, when we assert the existence of God, we are *not* asserting the existence of one more being, among others. What we are doing is hard to put. But once the distinction of III has been urged upon us, we are forced to face this matter squarely. Affirming the existence of God demands an uncanny reversal in our habitual way of thinking about existence, for it does not involve attributing to God the ordinary reality of those things with which we are most familiar, but letting that ordinary reality withdraw in the face of such extraordinary existence that it becomes true to say, as Anselm repeatedly does, that God alone exists.

The significance of this still may not be sufficiently striking, and this suggests that we have a way to go in understanding the conclusion of Anselm's argument. In fact, the note upon which III closes intimates the need for further clarification. Given the conclusion Anselm has drawn in this chapter the question arises;

Cur itaque 'dixit insipiens in corde suo: non est deus', cum tam in promptu sit rationali menti te maxime omnium esse? Cur, nisi quia stultus et insipiens?

Why then did "the Fool say in his heart: God does not exist," when it is so evident to a rational mind that You of all things exist to the highest degree? Why indeed, unless because he was stupid and a Fool?

This is the first mention of the Fool's claim that God does not exist since the beginning of II. Interestingly enough, it is presented as part of a question. Actually, there are more questions here than might be immediately apparent, and the most significant one is the most hidden. That is the question: What is it for something to be "evident" (*in promptu*) to a rational mind, and by what means is a matter brought forth (*promo*) in its evidence? Mention of this foreshadows the heart of the next chapter. And even the question that leads us to that discussion is not as pronounced as it could be. That is because we may have forgotten what it means to claim that something "exists to the highest degree' (*maxime omnium esse*). We have found this to mean no less than that it so exists that it cannot be thought not to exist. Now it surely seems that Anselm himself has a problem, despite the distractingly conclusive attitude toward the Fool in the last line. For it may be that the Fool is stupid to have claimed that God does not exist since Anselm claims to have shown that God truly exists; but Anselm looks a little foolish himself: He has shown that God cannot be thought not to exist, and the question naturally arises, then, how the Fool (indeed, any of us) is capable of thinking "*non est deus.*" This is no idle matter, nor a merely rhetorical question. If it were Anselm would not have devoted the whole of Chapter IV to its discussion. Possibly we can stress the force of his problem by transposing the apparent meaning of the last two lines into the following question: How can Anselm show something cannot be thought that even a stupid fool can think? How, indeed?

Chapter 3

Proslogion IV

Proslogion IV is, and has been, the more widely ignored aspect of Anselm's argument. One might think the reason for this obvious: IV appears to be nothing more than an appendix to the argument proper, that is, it does not seem to be part of the formal structure of the argument, but instead an attempt to overcome a predicament that the reasoning of II and III may have gotten us into. There is no doubt that IV does confront a certain problem that seems to follow from II and III, but in so doing it completes the argument. For it is Chapter IV that tells us how II and III are to be understood, and how the Fool is to be answered. In this way, IV is an integral part of the argument in so far as it explains what the reasoning of II and III has shown. And it is imperative that we listen to this explanation and not presume to already know what the argument demonstrates; for this is precisely what the chapter will instruct us in.

The title of IV runs:

Quomodo insipiens dixit in corde, quod cogitari non potest.

How the Fool said in his heart what cannot be thought.

and the first line of the chapter begins to develop an apparent problem:

Verum quomodo dixit in corde quod cogitare non potuit; aut quomodo cogitare non potuit quod dixit in corde, cum idem sit dicere in corde et cogitare?

But how has he said in his heart what he could not think; or how could he not think what he said in his heart, since to say in one's heart and to think are the same?

It is clear that IV begins with reference back to II and III. In II the Fool said in his heart that God does not exist; but by means of the argument of II and III, Anselm has shown that God truly exists, that is, so exists that He cannot be thought not to exist. But if, as Anselm here claims (and as we shall see in greater detail later) it is the same to think and say in the heart, then he does appear to have gotten himself into a rather perplexing position; for if the Fool said in his heart what cannot be thought, then the Fool thought what cannot be thought. Then either he thought what he could not think, or else did not think what he said he thought.

The most tempting evasion of this problem is to follow the second alternative. This, however, is not the move Anselm makes. Here it might be helpful to notice something. The question posed in the first line of IV is *not* the question posed in the title, indeed, the title of the chapter is not a question at all. It reads:

Quomodo insipiens dixit in corde, quod cogitari non potest.

This "*quomodo*" of the chapter heading is not to be understood in the same sense as the "*quomodo*" of the first line. For in the first line a question is posed, and so the "*quomodo*" is properly translated "*how*." In the title, however, there is no question asked. Rather, as with all the chapter headings, a claim is being made; a statement of what the chapter is to show. What this title claims the chapter shows is: *In what way* the Fool said in his heart what cannot be thought.[57] This "in what way" ("*quomodo*") corresponds to a claim that will soon be made to the effect that there is not only one way ("*non uno tantum modo*") in which something is thought. And it is precisely this distinction between the way the Fool thinks the matter at issue and another way, that pervades the entirety of IV and is its central consideration.

I make this point about the difference between the "*quomodo*" of the first line and the "*quomodo*" of the title, that is, between *asking how* the Fool thought what cannot be thought, and *claiming* to be able to show *in what way* the Fool thought what cannot be thought, because I believe the confusion of these has contributed to the neglect of IV. What one tends to assume when understanding the title as if it were the question of the first line is that the answer to the question: How did the fool think what cannot be thought? is simply that he never thought it at all. This assumption, however, is entirely mistaken. It could not be more mistaken. For precisely what the title of IV announces, when properly understood, and what this chapter claims to be able to show, is *in what way* the Fool thought what cannot be thought, which indicates that there is some way in which this can be thought. At this point it may seem like a paradox to say: there is a way in which one can think what cannot be thought; and yet, this is exactly what we must come to understand.

Not only is it wrong to assume that the Fool did not think this (i.e. that God does not exist) but it runs counter to what Anselm himself says in the very next line:

> *Quod si vere, immo quia vere et cogitavit quia dixit in corde, et non dixit in corde quia cogitare non potuit: non uno tantum modo dicitur aliquid in corde vel cogitatur.*

But if he really (indeed, since he really) both thought because he said in his heart and did not say in his heart because he could not think: there is not only one sense in which something is said in the heart or thought.

For some reason, Charlesworth decides in his translation to put in parentheses what I take to be a most crucial aspect of this line. This is no mere parenthetical remark, but is essential to the exact argument being made out here. For it is only on the basis of the claim that the Fool really did think this that Anselm grounds a distinction between two ways of thinking. Notice exactly how it is put. To be sure, the line begins with a *"si,"* that is, *"if."* But, as soon as Anselm says this, he takes it back. The *"immo"* tells us that by no means is it a matter of "if." This *"si"* is then immediately replaced by a *"quia"*: "because." Anselm is saying here: "if he really, no, on the contrary, because he really . . . ," in other words, he is explicitly accepting that the Fool really did think that God does not exist, and he seems to be willing to assert this as grounds for drawing a distinction between two ways of thinking.

On the basis of the Fool's assertion that God does not exist, not because he wants to deny that the Fool thought this, but because he accepts that he did, Anselm concludes that there is not only one way in which something can be thought. This is the only alternative if two claims, which seem to contradict one another, are both to stand. There must be one way in which the Fool can think that God does not exist and another, different way in which God cannot be thought not to exist. This would dissolve the paradox. For given that there are two ways in which something can be thought, to say that the Fool thought what cannot be thought would now mean: the Fool thought (in one way) what cannot be thought (in another way).

The difference between these two ways of thinking is set down in a manner that Anselm loves to make use of in presenting formal distinctions:

> *Aliter enim cogitatur res cum vox eam significans cogitatur, aliter cum id ipsum quod res est intelligitur.*

> For in one sense a thing is thought when the word signifying it is thought, in another sense when that which the thing itself is is understood.

It is important to recognize that this distinction is not *ad hoc*, that is, has not been introduced only for the sake of solving this particular problem. Nor is this sort of distinction peculiar to Anselm; it had been made before him by Augustine, and would be made after him by Thomas Aquinas.[58] Moreover, a similar distinction had already been made by Anselm himself in his first book, and not at a point at which he was attempting to avoid a problem, but in the midst of a discussion of the Supreme Nature. After having argued in *Monologion* IX that an example, or model, or principle of created things exists in the thought (*ratio*) of the Creator before creation, Anselm goes on, in subsequent chapters, to attempt to explicate further the nature of this thought (*ratio*). The opening section of *Monologion* X reads:

> *Illa   autem   rerum   forma,   quae   in   eius   ratione   res   creandas*

praecedebat: quid aliud est quam rerum quaedam in ipsa ratione locutio veluti cum faber facturus aliquod suae artis opus prius illud intra se dicit mentis conceptione? Mentis autem sive rationis locutionem hic intelligo, non cum voces rerum significativae cogitantur, sed cum res ipsae vel futurae vel iam existentes acie cogitationis in mente conspiciuntur. Frequenti namque usu cognoscitur, quia rem unam tripliciter loqui possumus. Aut enim res loquimur signis sensibilibus, id est quae sensibus quae foris sensibilia sunt, intra nos insensibiliter cogitando; aut nec sensibiliter nec insensibiliter his signis utendo, sed res ipsas vel corporum imaginatione vel rationis intellectu pro rerum ipsarum diversitate intus in nostra mente dicendo. Aliter namque dico hominem, cum eum hoc nomine, quod est 'homo', significo; aliter, cum idem nomen tacens cogito; aliter, cum eum ipsum hominem mens aut per corporis imaginem aut per rationem intuetur. Per corporis quidem imaginem, ut cum eius sensibilem figuram imaginatur; per rationem vero, ut cum eius universalem essentiam, quae est animal rationale mortale, cogitat.

But this model of things, which preceded their creation in the thought of the Creator, what else is it than a kind of expression of these things in his thought itself; just as when an artisan is about to make something after the manner of his craft, he first expresses it to himself through a concept? But by the expression of the mind or reason I understand, here, not when the words signifying the things are thought, but when the things themselves either future or already existing, by the vision of thinking are contemplated in the mind. For from frequent usage, it is recognized that we can express the same thing in three ways. For we express a thing either by the sensible use of sensible signs, that is, signs which can be sensed by bodily senses; or by thinking within ourselves insensibly these signs, which when outwardly used, are sensible; or not by employing these signs, either sensible or insensibly, but by expressing the things themselves inwardly in our minds either by imagination of the body or understanding of reason, according to the diversity of these things themselves. For I express a man in one way when by this name, which is 'man', I signify him; in another way, when I think this name silently; in another way, when the mind intuits the man himself either through the image of the body, or through reason. By means of the image of the body, for example, as when it imagines his sensible figure; by means of reason, however, as when it thinks his universal essence, which is rational mortal animal.[59]

In this well-known passage Anselm attempts to distinguish a number of different senses in which a thing can be expressed or said. Evidently, he is employing the notion of expressing (saying) in some unique ways. Most notable is its use in the phrase "expression of the mind or reason" (*mentis sive rationis locutionem*). This manner of saying is distinct from speaking by means of signs in that it gives expression to the thing itself by means of the vision of thinking (*acie cogitationis*). This should strike us as a peculiar matter, for we rarely understand "saying" in this sense. And yet such a manner of expressing the thing itself is just what we need to enquire into if we are to clarify the notion of "saying in the heart" as it is dealt with in *Proslogion* IV.

A distinction then has been drawn between a manner of saying in which signs are employed and a manner of saying in which they are not. In the former case, there is yet another distinction to be made, as in the latter. For signs, we are told, can be employed either sensibly or insensibly: they can be spoken externally so as to affect bodily senses, or they can be insensibly employed, that is, silently spoken within ourselves. This latter case Anselm treats as an example of thinking, or saying in the heart. He refers to it quite explicitly as "silently thinking" (*tacens cogito*). In this way of "saying in the heart," we employ a sign (silently within ourselves) in order to think about a thing. Evidently, Anselm is stressing the signifying character of signs; signs are utensils which are used (*utendo*) for the sake of signifying things. So, there is a sense in which *a thing* can be thought (about) by means of the sign which signifies it. This, however, is not to think the thing itself in the manner we must now look into.

Within that way of thinking the thing in which signs are not employed (*nec sensibiliter nec insensibiliter his signis utendo*) there is also a distinction to be made; for one can entertain the thing itself by means of bodily imagination or by means of rational understanding. Nothing seems unusual about the first case, and we should have no difficulty seeing its difference from the other sort of thinking (by means of signs), especially if we attend to Anselm's example. For, as he claims, thinking about a man by means of signs is not the same as beholding the man

himself in imagination. In the latter case, I do not mediate my relationship by employing signs, but intuit the man directly; I observe his "sensible figure" in imagination. Here I contemplate his corporeal image
"according to the diversity of the things themselves" (*pro rerum
ipsarum diversitate*), for when I entertain the sensible image of a man, I
do so according to that man's body, and so am guided in my intuition
of the matter by the matter itself.[60]

This, however, is only the first way of expressing a thing without the
use of signs. It is the other way that Anselm is most interested in; a
way distinct from thinking by means of signs as well as from imagining.
This is the way of intuiting a thing by means of rational understanding.
As with imagination, Anselm treats this as a way of intuiting a particular thing, and according to the characteristics peculiar to the thing
itself. We know that this is the crucial case of "expressing" or "saying"
(in the heart) developed in *Monologion* X, because it seems to refer us
to that "*mentis sive rationis locutionem*" which beholds the thing itself
in the vision of thinking. Such a saying or expressing of the thing in
thought is achieved by means of reason when a matter is intuited with
regard to its essential being (*essentia*). A man, for example may be
intuited in light of his "*universal essence*" which, according to Anselm,
is to be a rational mortal animal. Now this is quite different from
thinking (about) a man by means of signs, or imagining his body in that
we gain access to the essential reality of the thing. We must be clear,
however, that it is *the man himself* we intuit when we think *his* universal essence, in that reason is to give us access to the things themselves
(*rerum ipsarum*). And it is this winning of access to reality by rational
intuition which Anselm calls *understanding*.

This last way of thinking or saying (in the heart) is considered the
most fundamental; but, as we have seen, it is not the only activity
which can be legitimately characterized as "thinking." To be sure,
Anselm treats as a way of thinking (*cum eius universalem essentiam . . .
cogitat*) that most primary "word" which is "said in the heart" by
means of reason's intuition of the thing itself.[61] But he also seems to
consider as a case of thinking that manner of thinking about a thing by
means of the sign signifying it, in which signs are insensibly employed
within ourselves, and he specifically refers to this as "silently thinking"
(*tacens cogito*). Our inspection of this passage, then, quite simply and
unquestionably reveals that there is a definite ambiguity in the notion

of "thinking" or "saying in the heart" and it is this ambiguity which is reflected in *Proslogion* IV.

Looking back to the formal distinction of IV, we should be able to see that issues we have been discussing are, in certain respects, even reflected in the language of that distinction. For there we are told:

Aliter enim cogitatur res cum vox eam significans cogitatur, aliter cum id ipsum quod res est intelligitur.

On the one hand a thing is thought when the word signifying it is thought, on the other when that which the thing itself is is understood.

One can say that a thing is thought (about) when the sign signifying it is thought; but, in a more fundamental sense, a thing is thought when it itself is understood. We are distinguishing here two different ways of *thinking a thing*. In either case we aim to think *the thing*; in the one way by means of signs, in the other by *understanding* that which the thing itself is. The former way clearly refers to that "*tacens cogito*" in which the signs are insensibly employed; while the latter to that (reason's) intuitive vision of the thing itself which Anselm calls understanding. There is, however, a striking difference in the latter case. While in *Monologion* X Anselm characterized this intuition of the thing as reason's grasping of its "universal essence" (*universalem essentiam*), he speaks here of understanding "that which the thing itself is" (*id ipsum quod res est*). This is an important difference which we must now consider. So although *Monologion* X can be some help in clarifying the formal distinction, it cannot be substituted for a careful consideration of this distinction as it occurs in IV and so bears on the argument of II and III.

In the formal distinction of *Proslogion* IV Anselm does not speak of "universal essence" although he does speak of "understanding", which, as we have found, signifies reason's grasp of a singular thing. Such an intuition of singular things in certain cases (as in the case of a man) comprehends the universal essence of the thing. In IV, however, where we are to be speaking of God, Anselm characterizes reason's grasp as of "that which the thing itself is" (*id ipsum quod res est*). The *Proslogion*'s way of putting the matter seems to stress singularity rather than universality, although we should be clear that even in intuiting the universal essence of a thing, reason is aiming to comprehend a singular thing, though not in its singularity *per se*, but in what Anselm thought to be its greatest reality, that is, in its participation in a form (that *"rerum forma"* which begins the discussion in *Monologion* X) which could be shared by many possible individuals. So in comprehending the universal essence of a thing, it is the singular thing itself which is grasped, even if not in its unique singularity. Indeed, one may ordinarily think it characteristic of reason to attend to the universal dimension of a thing while neglecting its singularity.

This may be true, ordinarily. It is not true, however, in the extraordinary case of God. For, if it may be put this way, properly speaking God does not have a universal essence. This does not mean that reason has no access to God. Quite the opposite: it is reason alone that makes access to God possible.[62] Instead, to say that God has no *universal* essence is to remind us that given His essential description, there is one and only one possible individual that can fulfil that description. In the case of God, then, reason encounters no rift between the essential determination (in other cases, universal) and the singularity of the thing itself. For reason has the power to distinguish God *in His singularity* by means of an essential intuition. Here more than in any other case, reason can win access to that which the thing itself is, and in such a way that it can attain to the thing in its singular reality. This would seem a unique situation for reason to find itself in, and yet one might think that it is precisely in this case that reason attains its ownmost reality.

We are still a way from appreciating the power Anselm claims for reason with respect to understanding God. It should be more than evident, however, that the formal distinction between two ways of thinking has opened up issues which we might have missed entirely had we not inspected *Proslogion* IV carefully. For Anselm has now made quite clear that there is a way of thinking in which the thing itself is caught sight of by means of reason's vision, and that this way of thinking is radically different from the ordinary sort of thinking by means of signs as well as from the other way of entertaining the thing itself; that is, by imagining. This way of thinking we may simply call understanding. But now we have found that there is even for rational understanding a unique case, radically different from all others, and that this unique case is just the case in point: God. As in other cases, to be sure, such understanding brings us to an essential insight into the matter itself. In the case of God, however, the thing we are aiming to understand most fully allows for a grasp of that which the thing is, in so far as reason's vision has the capacity to win access to the singularity of the thing itself. The demand for such thinking, then, puts reason in an extremely exacting situation, and its rigor must be equal to the capability being claimed for it.

The important issue still facing us is exactly how this distinction between ways of thinking made in IV can be brought to bear on (our interpretation of) the reasoning of II and III. This question is explicitly answered by the conclusion of IV; but the very next line following the one under consideration places the distinction back into the context of the issue immediately pressing upon us: the question of the existence of God. For in that line Anselm announces that:

> *Illo itaque modo potest cogitari deus non esse, isto vero minime. Nullus quippe intelligens id quod deus est, potest cogitare quia deus not est, licet haec verba dicat in corde, aut sine ulla aut cum aliquia extranea significatione.*

In the first way, then, God can be thought not to exist, but not at all in the second. No one, indeed, understanding that which God is can think that God does not exist, even though he may say these words in his heart either without any or with some extraneous signification.

Certainly, the "understanding" referred to here must be read in terms of the specific notion of understanding we have been developing. In fact, the concluding line actually applies the formal distinction between two ways of thinking or saying in the heart to the particular case in point. For the reference to *id quod deus est* (that which God is) is simply an application of the formal way of putting the matter, *id ipsum quod res est* (that which the thing itself is), in the case in which the *res* (the matter to be understood) is *deus*. We could flesh out the phrase *id quod deus est* to read *id (ipsum) quod res* (i.e., *deus*) *est* to make this evident. The reference is, then, without question to that manner of intuiting the thing itself which is called understanding, and the line claims that no one understanding God, that is, enjoying essential intuition into the matter itself, can think that God does not exist. At the same time Anselm is immediately willing to admit that there are ways of thinking in which it is possible to think that God does not exist, ways other than that very exacting manner of contemplating the thing itself. We may, for example, simple fail to gain access to the *verbum cordis* and, consequently, fail to think the matter itself in any way whatsoever (saying in the heart without any signification) or, even if we do attempt to think the thing in the strictest sense, we may miss the mark and think something other than the very thing which it is (saying in the heart with some foreign signification). In either event, it becomes possible to think that God does not exist.

What it is incumbent upon us to appreciate, however, is not the manner in which we can fail to think the thing itself but to arrive at an appreciation of exactly what it is to succeed in understanding that which God is, and so be unable to think that God does not exist. This requires that even as we were now aiming to apply the formal distinction between two ways of thinking to the line under consideration, we should amplify that effort and attempt to apply it to the whole of the argument of II and III. Only in this way can we come to an adequate account of the force of that argument.

In fact, this is just what Anselm does in the lines which follow in IV. It is there that we encounter the essence of his argument.

> *Deus enim est id quo maius cogitari non potest. Quod qui bene intelligit, utique intelligit id ipsum sic esse, ut nec cogitatione queat non esse. Qui ergo intelligit sic esse deum, nequit eum non esse cogitare.*

> For God is that than which a greater cannot be thought. Whoever really understands this understands clearly that this same being so exists that not even in thought can it not exist. Thus whoever understands that God exists in such a way cannot think of Him as not existing.

Strikingly, "*intelligit*" is employed at least three times in the last two lines, and is from the beginning strengthened and stressed by adding "*bene*". We are speaking here of one who *really understands*; who well understands; indeed, who rightly understands. Can there be any doubt that "understands" is employed with "really" to emphasize that extra-

ordinary way of thinking in which one attains insight into the thing itself by means of the vision of reason and, therefore, that Anselm is
demanding something more than nominal understanding of the matter;
that in effect, he is claiming that such nominal thinking can never
approach the heart of the reasoning of II and III?

This critical passage encompasses the entirety of Anselm's argument.
It begins recalling the first step in the reasoning of *Proslogion* II: God
is *id quo maius cogitari non potest*. Now, whoever *really* understands
this, that is, that God is something than which nothing greater can be
thought, well understands that *id ipsum sic esse ut nec cogitatione
queat non esse*; that it itself so exists that it cannot be thought not to
exist. This latter claim is the conclusion which we have determined is
supposed to follow from the single argument of II and III. This clearly
indicates that the answer Anselm is offering (to the Fool's "*non est
deus*" of II) does not appeal to the conclusion of II, but to a conclusion
which is only stated in III and can be shown to follow not from the
reasoning of III alone, but from the single argument which spans II and
III. But something else is noteworthy here. In that the repeated use of
"*intelligit*" refers us to the strict manner of thinking in which the very
thing itself is grasped, our reading of the "*id ipsum*" should be enlight-
ened. For it formally recalls that way of thinking in which *id ipsum*
(*quod res est*) *intelligitur*. In accord with the conditions set down in IV,
then, that which the thing itself is (in this case, *id quod deus est*) must
be on display in this line; in which event, we should be treating the "*id
ipsum sic esse*" to be claiming that: it (the thing) itself so exists that it
cannot be thought not to exist. This would clarify our reading of the
entire passage. For it begins by claiming that God is something than
which nothing greater can be thought, and immediately turns to the
issue of what it is really to understand this *id quo maius cogitari non
potest*; that is, in that to understand signifies: to grasp the thing
itself (by means of reason's intuitive vision). The second line, then,
tells us that when this something than which a greater cannot be
thought is so understood, it is clearly seen that it (the thing) itself so
exists that it cannot be thought not to exist. And, finally, that whoever
has such sure insight into the matter itself cannot think that it does not
exist.

This may sound plain enough; but if taken to heart involves more
than is revealed in what we have said so far. We have yet to see exactly

what it would be to interpret the reasoning of II and III by appropriating it to the way of understanding which involves reason's vision of the thing itself. For this passage tempers the entire argument by repeatedly reminding us that it must be read in light of the sort of understanding distinguished in IV.

A number of hints have been given by Anselm himself, and certain matters already dealt with may assist us in accomplishing such a reading. Indeed, this very passage from IV makes abundantly clear that the reasoning of II and III is to give us access to the thing itself; that is to say, is to afford us understanding. And what it is we have been brought to understand by means of reasoning is the conclusion of that reasoning, a conclusion stated in III and repeated in IV: something than which nothing greater can be thought (God) so exists that it cannot be thought not to exist. This is the essential insight into the matter itself which the reasoning offers; the understanding of that which the thing itself is which is demanded if we are not to think that God does not exist. But reason's insight into the matter is unique in this case, for the essential intuition of God as that which so exists that it cannot be thought not to exist does not disclose a "universal essence" but rather distinguishes God from all else, and in so doing *directs reason's vision to the matter in its distinct singularity*.

Such "vision", of course, does not refer to the corporeal intuition of images by the imagination;[63] that is, it does not refer to "imaginative vision," but to the radically purified vision of the *oculus mentis* which gained insight into its matter, in this case, by means of the thoughtful distinction between what so exists that it cannot be thought not to exist and what so exists that it can be thought not to exist; *the* difference between God and everything else. Now, by the end of the last chapter we had shown how the claim that God so exists that He cannot be thought not to exist was to be distinguished from the claim that something exists both in the understanding and in reality. In the latter case, we tend to have creaturely existence in mind and this tends to mislead until it is sufficiently clarified by discriminating what so exists that it can be thought not to exist from what, to put it compactly, truly exists. We found, in this connection, that Anselm consistently held the view that with regard to this "singularly wonderful and wonderfully singular" way of existing, it is true to say that God alone exists; indeed, that compared to this existence which is God's (alone), all other things do not exist. The "so exists that it cannot be thought not to exist" as the distinctive mark (*proprium*) of God, we saw, expresses all of this.

It does, however, even more; and this is why it is so apt to accomphish the job it is called upon to do. For concealed within the phrase is a contemplative's prescription for thinking God. Against the strict measure of what so exists that it cannot be thought not to exist all other beings pale, as if to nothing. And the contemplative's task is to *perform* this annulment of existing creatures so that they may fade from reason's sight. For it is through this withdrawal of all creatures that the way is cleared for *a radically purified* (rational) *vision of the matter itself*, that is, of something than which nothing greater can be thought. This vision over-passes all those things which can be thought not to exist until it comes to rest upon that which alone truly exists, in its singularity and precisely as that which *sic esse ut nec cogitatione queat non esse*.

In treating the "so exists that it cannot be thought not to exist" as at one and the same time both reason's revelation of God and a contemplative's prescription for thinking God (and these belong together), it should be evident that I am trying to re-implant the argument in its native soil; that is, to recommend that Anselm's argument has its roots, and therefore its life, in the practice of contemplation. The evidence for this is abundant. It is well-known that Anselm himself, in his introduction to the *Proslogion*, after expressing the hope that his argument might bring to others the joy it brought him, explains that he therefore wrote it: *sub persona conantis erigere mentem suam ad contemplandum deum*,[64] in the person of one striving to elevate his (own) mind to contemplate God. This "elevation" is just the movement of thinking we have been attempting to characterize in which the mind elevates itself above all creatures in order to behold God. Such a movement is one that each performs on his own; presumably by means of the practice of contemplation and with the assistance of Anselm's argument.

It is this sort of contemplative activity, then, which is being signaled by the repeated employment of "*intelligit*" in these lines which encapsule the whole of the argument of II and III, and it is the one who has effected the movement toward God that is referred to as "one who really understands." It is this one alone who, as we are told in the third line, cannot think that God does not exist. For in so far as an essential intuition into the matter has been won, and in so far as this way of thinking is determined by the matter itself (*pro rerum ipsarum diver-sitate*) such understanding is binding upon thought. The one who well understands that God is that than which a greater cannot be thought is the one who, in attempting to think (contemplate) the matter has come to see (by means of the vision of reason) that such a being so exists that it cannot be thought not to exist. That is to say, by following an argu-ment which shows that God truly exists, something which so exists that it cannot be thought not to exist has been brought into view. And whoever has caught sight of that which alone exists in this way, cannot think that it does not exist. This, however, is true only of the one who "really understands," and true only at the contemplative moment at which thinking accedes to the matter itself. Were one to lose sight of the matter, it would again become possible to think that God does not exist.

These three lines which, shall we say, condense the whole of Anselm's argument into a final flurry of thinking draw together so much that we may encounter no little difficulty keeping it all straight. None-theless, there is no doubt that they alone hold Anselm's answer to the Fool; an answer which shows a great deal of understanding not only of the matter at issue, but of the needs of those who might put the exis-tence of God in question. And this answer is not, as one might imagine if the last two lines of III are misread, that the Fool is simply stupid in claiming he thought what cannot be thought (to wit: that God does not exist). For even were this the case, it would still be imperative to display in exactly what such "stupidity" consists. In fact, the Fool is not mentioned in IV after the formal distinction between two ways of thinking. We can, I believe, make the most of this by looking back to the last mention of the Fool and even before the conclusion of III. That mention is early on in II and, interestingly enough, during a dis-cussion of what he understands of "*aliquid quo nihil maius cogitari possit.*" There we are told that the Fool "understands" something than which nothing greater can be thought because:

   . . . hoc cum audit intelligit . . .

   . . . he understands this when he hears it . . .

We saw, following Anselm's own reply, that "understand" was here being used in a weak sense. The sort of understanding that the Fool has is not a matter of thinking that which the thing itself is, but simply involves thinking (in the weakest sense of that term) about the thing by means of the words that one hears. Indeed, this sense of "understand" seems to correspond exactly to the weaker sense of "think" that is presented in IV, in which one thinks the sign signifying the thing without in any way understanding (in the strong sense) the thing itself. And yet, even as this weaker sense of "thinking" a thing is rejected in IV as inadequate for a proper understanding of the matter at hand, it appears, as this quote from II should indicate, to be the very starting point of Anselm's own argument. Precisely the way in which II characterizes what the Fool "understands" is to say that he "understands what he hears" (*intelligit quod audit*); that is to say, he understands the words that he hears in so far as he speaks the language.

This, I hope, brings into prominence the following crucial point: if Anselm's argument begins in II by simply thinking in the weak sense the sign signifying the thing, and ends in IV demanding that one think, in the strongest sense, that which the thing itself is (*id ipsum quod res est intelligitur*), then this must mean that the aim and strategy of the argument involves the *development of understanding*. For certainly the reasoning of II and III must supply us with the understanding which is demanded in IV, and this turns out to be nothing less than access to the matter itself, in this case, to *id quod deus est*. As we have already seen, the conclusion of the single argument of II and III does offer us exactly this, since it shows that something than which nothing greater can be thought (God) is that which so exists that it cannot be thought not to exist. This is just what is brought into view for one who "really understands" the argument. And so although we may begin with merely nominal understanding, our following of the argument should unfold the sort of understanding which claims insight into the matter itself; that is, into God.[65]

In connection with this sort of understanding the Fool is not mentioned, for his thinking remains on the level at which it began. In effect, then, Anselm's argument does not really concern the Fool, least of all does it aim to convince him of anything. To think this would simply be to confuse the one the argument is directed *against* with the one the argument is designed *for*. There can be no doubt that Anselm's concern lies with those who are "striving to elevate their (own) mind to contemplate God,"[66] and the strategy of his argument, as I have interpreted it, involves the development of the sort of understanding which is properly characterized as an elevation of the mind toward God. It is this movement which rests at the heart of Anselm's argument, and to which the Fool has no access.

It is little wonder, then, that in the concluding prayer of IV, which thanks the Lord for understanding, Anselm himself is declared the recipient:

> *Gratias tibi, bone domine, gratias tibi, quia quod prius credidi te donante, iam sic intelligo te illuminante, ut si te esse nolim credere, non possim non intelligere.*

> I give thanks, good Lord, I give thanks to You, since what I believed through Your free gift I now so understand through your illumination, that if I did not want to believe that You existed, I should nevertheless be unable not to understand it.

Contained in this passage is a paradoxical reversal of the often quoted line which immediately precedes *Proslogion* II: *"nisi credidero, non intelligam"*; "unless I believe, I shall not understand."[67] Here in IV Anselm proclaims that even if he did not believe, he should nevertheless be unable not to understand. Presumably, this marks the binding character of such "illumination," an illumination for which one is prepared by the reasoning of II and III and which has shed so much light on the matter that Anselm is willing to claim that even without faith the existence of God would be evident. Such "evidence" was mentioned at the close of III when we were told that "it is evident to a rational mind" (*in promptu sit rationali menti*) that God truly exists. We now have a way of saying what this bringing forth before (*promo*) the rational mind amounts to. The illumination of which Anselm speaks is reason's revelation of God as He is brought before the mind by the purified vision of thinking. This illumination, which the argument claims to afford, provides the light by which the matter itself may be seen (*video*) and so brought forth in its own evidence (*evidens*) as that which alone truly exists. And since the matter at issue has been brought into view, even one who does not believe should nevertheless understand.

The argument ends as it began: with a prayer. This concluding line formally complements the opening prayer of II, for the *"Ergo domine . . . da mihi"* parallels the *"Gratias tibi, bone domine"*; the original prayer was petitionary, while the prayer that concludes IV thanks God for having granted the requests made in that opening line of II. The final prayer of IV, then, announces the completetion of the argument in so far as the consummation of the original petition has been granted. But exactly what this original request was, and in what way it has been fulfilled, we will not be clear about until we have returned to the opening line of II and examined it in greater detail.

Chapter 4

Conclusion

We must now return to the beginning. An issue yet remains to be discussed that was left undecided from the start; in fact, from the very first line of the argument. I said at that point, in the earliest phase of II, that we would not be in a position to interpret this line until after having worked our way through the entire argument. We have now achieved this, and are prepared to conclude our study by returning to that opening line.

Proslogion II begins:

Ergo, domine, qui das fidei intellectum, da mihi, ut quantum scis expedire intelligam, quia es sicut credimus et hoc es quod credimus.

Therefore, Lord, You who give understanding to faith, grant me that I may understand, as much as you see fit, that You exist as we believe and that You are that which we believe.

Certain issues raised here are brought into prominence thanks to the discussion of *Proslogion* IV. One issue, which we have already mentioned in our initial encounter with this line, centers around the concluding portion, which reads in Latin:

. . . quia es sicut credimus et hoc es quod credimus.

We said that many have taken this petition to mark a dual purpose operating in the *Proslogion* as a whole. On the one hand, so it has been argued, Anselm wants to show that God exists (. . . *quia es sicut credi-mus*) and, on the other, he wants to show what God is (. . . *et hoc es quod credimus*). These interpreters have gone so far as to break up the text in accord with what they took to be distinct petitions, claiming that while one section of the *Proslogion* (Chapters II-IV) deals with the existence of God, the other (Chapters V-XXVI) deals with the essence of God. Some have disagreed, in principle, with this sort of breaking apart of the text, and have deviated from its basic intention; but, none-theless, I think it safe to say that almost all of Anselm's interpreters have acknowledged two quite different petitions in this line.[68]

After a careful inspection of IV, however, this view becomes inde-fensible. More than that, such an interpretation of the first line misses entirely the profundity and completeness of the single argument as it occurs in Chapters II and III of the *Proslogion*. Indeed, if I am correct, something is being announced in the first line concerning the aim of Anselm's argument which has not, to this day, been properly under-stood.

To be sure, Anselm begins by declaring a twofold purpose in his seeking. He seeks to understand that God exists "as we (the faithful) believe" and that God is "that which we believe." But nothing he says would indicate that these are separate petitions. In fact, they are an-nounced together, and the "*et*" which joins them accentuates this.

The essential togetherness of these two aims can be brought into focus by attending closely to the Latin. What is normally treated as the first petition asks to understand: *quia es sicut credimus*, that God exists as (*sicut*) we believe. This is usually taken to mean that we, the faithful, believe that God exists, and so Anselm is seeking to understand this; that is, that God exists. There is, however, a more careful reading suggested, if we take the "*sicut*" seriously.[69] For "*sicut*" can mean: just as, or in the same way as. On this reading, the line would be saying that Anselm seeks to understand that God exists *just as* the faithful be-lieve; exists *in the way* in which they believe. And in what "way" do the faithful believe God to exist? The answer to this is given in the title which immediately precedes the line under discussion: the faithful be-lieve that God truly exists (*Quod vere sit deus.*) And if, as I have argued, this means that God exists in a specific way, in a way in which he alone can; that He so (*sic*) exists that (*ut*) He cannot be thought not to exist, then it stands to reason that when Anselm prays for understanding he would request to understand the exact way of existing appropriate to God.

Once we realize that *"vere esse"* (in the title of II) when referred to God signifies a distinctive way of existing, it becomes apparent that the request to understand that God exists as the faithful believe asks to understand the exact way of existing in which God is believed to exist. This, however, should have direct bearing on our understanding of the second half of the petition; especially if we do not forget that *vere esse* is the distinctive character of God. For the second request asks to understand that God is that which the faithful believe (*hoc es quod credimus*). We have seen in our discussion of IV that the *id ipsum sic esse ut nec cogitatione queat non esse* is treated there as a disclosure of that which God is (*id quod deus est*). In fact, understanding that which God is, in IV, is presented as a requirement if one is not to think that God does not exist. Not only that: given the argument depends upon the development of such understanding (of *id quod deus est*) and that this is achieved by following the reasoning of II and III, which claims to show that God (is that which) truly exists, it is clear that these two requests cannot be separated if Anselm's argument is conclusively to succeed in its aim. Put in terms of this petition, we might say that Anselm claims to afford access to that which God is by means of a clear understanding of the exact way in which God exists and, in turn, understanding that which God is alone rules out the possibility of thinking that God does not exist. Consequently, understanding that God truly exists answers both petitions, for when the *"sicut"* of the first is heard properly, the two requests become one. Understanding *both* that God exists in just the way the faithful believe and that God is that which they believe comes down to understanding: *Quod vere sit deus*.

The emphatic plea for understanding made in this first line not only serves to confirm our position that at the heart of Anselm's argument lies the development of understanding, but elucidates the specific task involved in calling for such a movement. This need for understanding both echoes and is to be interpreted in light of the signification this term receives through its discussion in *Proslogion* IV, where genuine understanding (*bene intelligit*) consists in reason's vision of the matter itself (*id ipsum quod res est*). It is this which Anselm seeks (for himself as well as his reader) from the start; and no less so because we have neglected the line which announces it as irrelevant to the argument proper or failed to appreciate the strict meaning of "understand" intended there. For the very first line declares the argument's aim to bring us to a clear view of the (singular) existence of God and, at the same time, to a vision of the matter itself (*id quod deus est*); both of which are achieved in showing that God truly exists.

This opening line, then, *provides the interpretive key to Anselm's argument*; a key which had already been offered in the original title of the work: *Fides Quaerens Intellectum*: Faith Seeking Understanding. Philosophical understanding seeks reason's revelation of those matters already revealed to faith. In the case in point, that is, in the *Proslogion*, understanding seeks the highest object of faith—God—and it seeks to attain to reason's vision of this matter. Had we really begun at the beginning (of the *Proslogion*), we need not have waited until IV to appreciate the force of this. In fact, the "*Ergo*" which stands in front of this first line of II suggests that the chapter itself is to be placed in the context of something which has gone before. This can be nothing other than *Proslogion* I; a prayer aimed at inspiring contemplation of God, and which could offer no better account of what Anselm's seeking consists in and how, therefore, the text which follows is to be read. In this *Excitatio mentis ad contemplandum deum* Anselm is, from the outset, explicit about the nature of his venture:

> *Quaero vultum tuum,*
> *vultum tuum, Domine, requiro.*

> I seek your face,
> For Your face, Lord, I search.[70]

Not only is the object of his search clearly delimited here, but Anselm admits his need (*requiro*) to win a glimpse of the face of God. This alone will enlighten that darkness in which we, as "the miserable children of Eve", find ourselves:

> *Aerumnosi,*   *unde sumus expulsi,*
>   *quo sumus impulsi!*
>   *Unde praecipitati,*
>   *quo obruti!*
> *A patria in exsilium,*
> *a visione Dei in caecitatem nostram.*

> Poor wretches,   from where are we expelled,
>   to where are we impelled!
>   from where have we fallen,
>   to where have we plunged!
> From our homeland into exile,
> from the vision of God into our blindness.

We must not be misled by the fact that Anselm here speaks of our
"exile from the vision of God," for it is just such loss he prays to be
saved from. At this point, we are in the midst of a lament (*"universalis
planctus filorum Adae"*), but just a few lines later the transition is already beginning:

> *Et o tu, Domine, usquequo?*
> *Usquequo, Domine, oblivisceris nos,*
> *usquequo avertis faciem tuam a nobis?*
> *Quando respicies et exaudies nos?*
> *Quando illuminabis oculos nostros et ostendes nobis faciem*
>   *tuam?*
> *Quando restitues te nobis?*
> *Respice, Domine, exaudi, illumina nos, ostende nobis teipsum.*

> And You, O Lord, how long?
> How long, Lord, will you forget us,
> how long will You turn Your face from us?
> When will You look upon us and hear us?
> When will You illuminate our eyes and show to us Your face?
> When will You restore Yourself to us;
> Look upon us, Lord, hear us, illuminate us, show to us Yourself.

We have already found Anselm thanking the Lord for such illumination
in the concluding prayer of IV, after having seen *id* (*ipsum*) *quod deus
est*.   And in so far as this very understanding was connected with
reason's vision, there can be no doubt that it is the *oculus mentis* both
which Anselm here asks to be illuminated and which is, in the earlier
passage, accounted "blind" in its failure to attain to the *"visione dei."*
In this latter passage, however, Anselm indicates that our "exile from
the vision of God into our blindness" is not inescapable, for he explic-

itly asks the Lord to "show . . . Yourself." This invocation is repeated just before the end of the prayer:

> *Liceat mihi suspicere lucem tuam,*
> *vel de longe,*
> *vel de profundo.*
> *Doce me quaerere te et*
> *ostende te quaerenti; quia*
> *nec quaerere te possum, nisi tu doceas,*
> *nec invenire,   nisi te ostendas.*

> Let me look upward to Your light,
> even if from afar,
> even if from the depths.
> Teach me to seek You, and
> show Yourself as I seek; because
> neither can I seek You, unless You teach,
> nor find,   unless You show Yourself.

Anselm seems to suggest here that he expects to be able to find what he is seeking, that is, a vision of the face of God, if only the Lord will show Himself. Presumably, in this life, such a vision is not "face to face", although it is of the thing itself, albeit from afar (*vel de longe*/*vel de profundo*). The entire chapter is replete with images of vision, of illumination, of God showing Himself. And this is exactly what faith seeks in so far as it seeks understanding; this is specifically what *fides quaerens intellectum* amounts to in this case. What Anselm consistently announces he is seeking is a vision of God, and it is by means of rational understanding (contemplation) that he hopes to attain to that vision.

All of this stands at the background of the opening line of II, and the "*Ergo*" which begins that line is stationed there as a reminder. Were one to think that the contemplative aim unfolded in *Proslogion* I referred to something later in the text, or something other than the argument of II and III, they need only recall that II begins with a condensed form of this invocation, and that it must be treated as setting the stage for what follows. In that first line Anselm requests the understanding which is granted to faith, and such understanding turns out to signify nothing less than a vision of God.

This, however, does *not* mean that Anselm's argument should be treated as an expression of mystical insight rather than as an effort of reason.[71] It does mean that the opening line of II must provide a clue as to how the argument is to be read *as an argument*; that is to say, we must let these considerations instruct us in exactly what an argument is on this account.   The procedure of reasoning which is Anselm's argument evolves the sort of understanding which admits reason to a vision of the matter itself. This reasoning, then, has shown the matter at issue just in so far as it has brought the matter itself into view. Now, to be sure, argument involves the establishment of a claim with evidence, and reason argues in so far as it adduces evidence. But, as we saw at the end of the last chapter, the clarity of vision reasoning affords lets the subject matter of the claim itself be seen in its ownmost evidence. It is something like this we must read Anselm to be requesting in the opening line of II and finally claiming to have achieved in the complementary prayer concluding IV, in which he thanks God for the "illumination."[72]   The single argument of II and III shows that God truly exists in so far as it brings into (reason's) view something which so exists that it cannot be thought not to exist, and rests on the claim that anyone who has (by following the argument) been shown the subject itself cannot think that God does not exist.

This claim I am making, that, in effect, Anselm's argument aims to fulfil the request made upon God in *Proslogion* I to "show Yourself" may seem incredible; all the more so if one recalls that in the *Monologion* he appears to deny this possibility. In his first book, supposed to have been written within a year of the *Proslogion*, Anselm argues that we cannot properly see God, that is, we cannot see the thing itself:

Et saepe videmus aliquid non proprie, quemadmodum res ipsa est, sed per aliquam similitudinem aut imaginem; ut cum vultum alicuius consideramus in speculo.

And often we see something not properly, as it is in itself, but through some likeness or image; as when we look upon a face in a mirror.[73]

Now this does characterize Anselm's approach in the *Monologion*; although we have already seen that we cannot depend upon this earlier work to clarify completely issues raised in the *Proslogion*. As a matter of fact, this would seem most true just at the point we are presently considering, since the traditional arguments for the existence of God rehearsed in the *Monologion* are altogether different *in kind* from the original argument of the *Proslogion*. Not only that: everything claimed in this passage contradicts claims developed in those early chapters of the *Proslogion* we have scrutinized. Here we are told that we cannot know God in terms of the characteristics peculiar to Him (*proprie*), that is, we are told we cannot see the thing itself (*res ipsa*), while in the *Proslogion* the "*non possit cogitari non esse*" is announced as the peculiar character of God (*proprium*), and what's more, reason's vision of the thing itself (*id ipsum quod res est*) is precisely what is demanded in IV. Anselm concludes (in accord with the sort of arguments offered in the *Monologion*) that the face (*vultum*) of God can only be seen in a mirror; in terms, that is, of its relative similarity to other things. In *Proslogion* I there is also talk of seeking a glimpse of the face (*vultum*) of God, only no mention is made of mirrors. And properly so, for the argument of II and III does not trade upon the similarity of God with other beings, but stresses His radical distinctiveness. To show that God truly exists in no way asserts a similitude between God and what can be thought not to exist nor does it depend upon one in so far as this distinctive characterization (i.e. *non possit cogitari non esse*) would retain its force even if there were no other beings. Indeed, it has such force that it is able to clear all other beings out of the way so that reason's vision is directed to the matter in its singularity.

This passage from the *Monologion*, then, seems to confute, at each point, claims we have seen unfold in the *Proslogion*. And it is the language which is telling. For Anselm not only contradicts himself, he asserts those contradictions using the very same words. And he is never loose in his language. Precisely the opposite: Anselm had a propensity for developing technical terminology. Could it be that this contrast does not so much mark a contradiction in Anselm's works as a transformation in his thinking which is expressly manifest in the very language in which it is declared? If so, then this means the discovery of his own (original) argument, which he tells us brought such joy, afforded him access to that which he thought himself barred from in his earlier work. This would explain the lofty request made upon God in *Proslogion* I to "show Yourself", to "illuminate our eyes", as well as the closing prayer of IV which thanks God for that illumination. For the anticipatory proposal in *Proslogion* I, to employ the reasoning which follows in the practice of contemplation, serves to indicate that the philosophical force of that argument is sufficient to offer a vision of God (as that which truly exists). The nature and significance of such vision is, of course, fully elaborated in *Proslogion* IV, when it is applied directly to the argument of II and III, although it is promised from the beginning. No other conclusion can account for the variety of issues we have seen emerge throughout our discussion. Only a proper understanding of the claim that Anselm's argument aims to offer a vision of God will allow us to appreciate the unity and completeness of the single argument from its opening line to its concluding prayer.

If this claim seems startling, it should; for it asks us to relinquish our right to an easy and, by now, habitual way of interpreting the argument. This was already becoming clear when, in order to account for its own conclusion, we needed to offer a new interpretation of the relation of II to III; but it runs deeper than this. For that account raised issues which could be settled only by inquiring into an aspect of the argument which sheds essential light on its reasoning, and yet has been all but universally neglected: *Proslogion* IV. And in that chapter, it seems to me, questions arise concerning the very *nature* of this argument. The matter of the relation between II and III is, certainly, a crucial one; but it achieves this critical stature only in so far as it serves to change our thinking about the argument by clarifying the full scope of its aim. Admittedly, my interpretation forces the emergence of issues we are not usually asked to consider in connection with Anselm's reasoning. It should, however, be clear by now that the strangeness presently confronting us does not lie simply in my account, but at the heart of the reasoning itself. It stems from the fact that Anselm's argument attempts to unite logical rigor with mystical insight; and we are not accustomed to the strenuous demand upon thinking such a seemingly unlikely union entails. Those who treat the argument as an expression of mysticism (independent of logical standards) miss this as surely as those who would deal with it as an exercise in logic. In Anselm these two dimensions are blended; for, on his account, *reason is the way to the vision of God*.

Along with the abandonment of traditional interpretations, we must resist the temptation to expect a certain habitual sort of evaluation; that is, we must also relinquish our right to an evaluation of this argu-

ment made easy by inspecting its discursive dimension while remaining
oblivious to the intuitive function it is designed to serve. Having been
keen to this difference (which *Monologion* X begins to make explicit
in mention of that rational intuition [*rationem intuetur*] referred to as
"understanding"), I have informally and rather loosely throughout
sought to imply a distinction between the reasoning proper and the
argument, and only in this conclusion finally clarified the meaning
of "argument." Put in these terms, it might be said that I have been
attempting to provide an analysis of Anselm's argument, not merely of
his reasoning. And once the nature of this argument comes clear, the
seemingly pressing need for a traditional evaluation pales in the face of
a more essential demand.[74] Ultimately, of course, we would like to
provide an evaluation of Anselm's argument; not however, only of his
reasoning. I have provided an analysis of neither in this work, although
we have been brought to the point from which we can see that deeper
schooling in this argument may be required before any sense might be
made of the kind of essential evaluation that is called for. The obliga-
tory observations concerning its discursive reasoning may only serve to
obscure the fact that a task of evaluation remains to be done, and one
of an essentially different sort than traditional considerations of the
argument seen to have noticed.

   Not only, then, do we conclude that Anselm's argument has never
been properly understood, but that its profound depth is not touched
by the sorts of surface evaluation it ordinarily receives. Now realizing
that the argument's fundamental strategy is to grant access to reason's
vision of God (to develop understanding), it should become an issue
how the evaluation of the argument is to proceed. Determining its logical validity is as inconclusive as sheltering it in mysticism. Nor will it
suffice to attempt to tie these two together *ex post facto*. Rather, in
so far as the argument is founded upon an original unity between reason and the vision of God, any consideration of its soundness must
determine to what extent its reasoning affords vision, as well as the sta-
tus such vision should enjoy. In order to achieve this, the argument
would have to be inspected with the same sort of detailed care that has
led us to what I claim to be its definitive account. For if the evaluation
of a philosophical argument must be equal to the thoughtfulness of the
argument itself, then, if I am correct about this argument, its definitive
evaluation may take as much effort to unfold as the argument itself has.

Such considerations help to mark the limits of the present work as an "introduction" to Anselm's argument, and to indicate the appropriateness of having concluded our discussion where it began; that is, with an account of the opening line of *Proslogion* II. For we have not aimed to arrive at any conclusion, if that means to have done at last with this celebrated argument. Quite the opposite. If we have been introduced to Anselm's argument, have even become acquainted with it in some measure, then in returning to the original we must be prepared to approach it with new appreciation. This would demand that we allow the argument a fresh beginning. In the end, it seems only necessary to appeal to this entire study as evidence that Anselm's argument cannot fairly be treated as a past event in the history of philosophy which we have been called upon to judge, but an argument which demands to be understood, and is still calling upon those who would attempt to think their own way through it to accomplish that task.

Notes

1. Norman Malcolm, "Anselm's Ontological Arguments," *Philosophical Review* LXIX, 1960, pp. 41-62. Reprinted in Alvin Plantinga, *The Ontological Argument*, New York, 1965.

2. D. P. Henry, "*Proslogion* Chapter 3," in *Analecta Anselmiana*, Band I, Frankfort, 1969; and *The Logic of St. Anselm*, Oxford, 1967.

3. R. LaCroix, *Proslogion II and III: A Third Interpretation of Anselm's Argument*, Leiden, 1972.

4. *Anselmi Opera Omnia*, ed. F. S. Schmitt, Stuttgart, 1968, vol. I, p. 123.

5. F. S. Schmitt, *Anselmi Opera Omnia*, Tomus I, p. 64: "Das Proslogion hatte zuerst weder Prooemium noch Kapitelverzeichnis (siehe die Hss. VHLIGEN) noch irgendeine Abteilung des Textes (siehe die Hss. VIGEN). Es war der Form nach ein Gebet. Der Titel aber, den Anselm zuerst gab (siehe sein späteres Prooemium), hebt es sofort uber den Rahmen des Gebetes hinaus: es wurde eine spekulative Schrift. Dies verlangte nach einer Einteilung des Textes mit einem vor dem Werke angebrachte Kapitelverzeichnis."

6. M. J. Charlesworth, *St. Anselm's* Proslogion, Oxford, 1965, p. 116/117. From this point on I will not footnote quotes from Anselm's Chapters II-IV of the *Proslogion*. I shall be employing throughout this work the Charlesworth translation, not without alteration, however. The more serious questions of translation I shall argue for within the work itself, as we come to them. Some general alterations I shall make throughout. For example, I shall render *esse in intellectu* as "exists in the understanding" rather than Charlesworth's "exists in the mind." I should also like to apologize for the inability to present a consistent

99

rendering of *esse*. At some points it will be translated as "to be" and at others "to exist." Rendering it as "exist" fails to distinguish it from *existere*, employed in the last line of II. For simplicity's sake, it is easiest to remember that except in the last line of II, whenever the word "exist" occurs in the argument, it translates *esse*.

7. Karl Barth, *Anselm: Fides Quaerens Intellectum*, tr. I. W. Robertson, Richmond, Virginia, 1958. The very first line of Barth's Introduction reads: "The Proof for the Existence of God comprises the first and disproportionately shorter of the two parts (cap. 2-4 and 4-26) of Anselm's *Proslogion*. The second and longer part goes on to deal with the Nature of God." (p. 13) A variation of this view is held by D. P. Henry in "*Proslogion* Chapter 3." At the very conclusion of his article, Henry states: "In *Proslogion* 2, the *existence* of God is in question (*es sicut credimus*); in *Proslogion* 3 the first of a whole series of attributes is being investigated (*hoc es quod credimus*) . . . " (p. 105).

8. *Anselmi Opera Omnia*, vol I., p. 104, note.

9. Barth, p. 77: "*Quo maius cogitari nequit* . . . is in fact as far as he (Anselm) is concerned a revealed Name of God." I don't mean that what I have said here is what Barth has in mind when he speaks of a "revealed Name" but it may be a way for philosophers to get a grasp of what I take to be an important point. There is a ground for this phrase in a tradition of thinkers who, in attempting to characterize and give voice to that which they sought, and in some measure understood, saw fit to use an expression very much like Anselm's own.

10. If Anselm had held such a principle, it would not have been peculiar to him, nor something appealed to *ad hoc*. In the 9th century, for example, Fredegisus had claimed that: "Omne itaque nomen finitum aliquid significat, ut homo, lapis, lignum. Haec enim ubi dicta fuerint, simul res quas fuerint significant intelligimus." Henry translates this: "Every finite name (e.g. 'man', 'stone', 'wood') signifies something. Whenever these happen to be spoken, immediately the things which are in question, and which they signify are understood." (For full quotation and translation see Henry, *The Logic of St. Anselm*, Oxford, 1967, p. 208). Obviously, what is being stressed here is the signifying character of signs; as we shall see Anselm himself do in *Proslogion* IV.

11. In fact, about as broad as the use of *aliquid* ("something") in ordinary language according to an account Anselm gives in *Eines neues unvollendetes Werk des hl. Anselm von Canterbury (Beiträge zur Geschichte der Philosophie und Theologie des Mittelalters* 3/33), Münster, 1936.

12. It is not clear that this general principle can, in the end, be maintained. Anselm elsewhere admits that it is *not* the same for something to be understood and for it to exist in the understanding (in *Eines neues unvollendetes Werk*, p. 43) and gives as an example indefinite nouns (like "not-man"). In this case, although "not-man" may be understood, we would not say that there is something (e.g. a concept) in the understanding (of "not-man"). This may seem like a rather bizarre counter-example, but it is at the same time possible that "something than which nothing greater can be thought" is of just such a sort.

13. Charlesworth, pp. 156/157-158/159; pp. 182/183-184/185.

14. I have recently found that A. Kolping discerns something very much like this and in discussion of Chapter II, claims: "Ein solcher intelligible Inhalt ist in mein Erkenntnis da. Damit sind aber noch zwei Möglichkeiten unentscheiden und offengelassen: Entweder ist dieses aliquod quo maius cogitari nequit bloss intelligibler Inhalt, vielleicht die Möglichkeit zu etwas Subsistentem, aber auch nicht mehr, oder der intelligible Inhalt ist auch irgendwo konkretisiert und subsistent, er 'existiert'." Adolf Kolping, *Anselms Proslogion-Beweis der Existenz Gottes (Grenzfragen zwischen Theologie und Philosophis*, vol. 7), Bonn, 1939, p. 69.

15. Charlesworth, p. 174/175.

16. We may seem obliged to discuss this principle since, in thinking it the pivotal point of the argument, commentators have given it by far the most attention. And while its role cannot be ignored there is no doubt that it has been unduly overemphasized. When its place in II is rightly understood, it becomes clear that it is *not* indispensable and, in fact, plays only a secondary part. For the claim that it is greater to exist both in the understanding and in reality than in the understanding alone is introduced only to justify the genuinely central point that for any X, if X exists in the understanding alone, a greater can be thought. But this latter claim could be justified otherwise. We might even appeal to the character at issue as valuable; that is, suggest that something which cannot exist in the understanding alone is greater than something which can. So if X exists in the understanding alone, a Y can be thought which cannot exist in the understanding alone, which is greater. This would serve as well to validate the claim Anselm presses: in effect, that if X exists in the understanding alone, a greater can be thought. I mention this not with an eye to defending Anselm (for the principle I have offered may be equally questionable) but to indicate the dispensability of the former principle. There is, however, another benefit to putting the matter this way, for in appealing to the principle that what cannot exist in the understanding alone is greater than what

can, we may see that it would not follow that X cannot exist in the understanding alone or, least of all, that X exists. All that would follow is that something greater can be thought than what exists in the understanding alone. I note this because somehow one suspects that Anselm imports existence in reality into his argument at this juncture where he claims that it is greater to exist than not to exist (and so one thinks this the place to come down on him.) When considered carefully, it is evident that he does not. Instead, this notorious claim is employed to show that whatever exists in the understanding alone is something than which a greater can be thought. See, in this connection, *Anselmi Opera Omnia*, vol. I, p. 101, *Priores recensiones* of line 16-17.

17. There is some reason to think that Thomas Aquinas may have helped to perpetuate this misunderstanding. See especially his presentation of the reasoning of II in *Summa Contra Gentiles*.

18. Charlesworth, p. 156/157.

19. Charlesworth, p. 178/179.

20. When I say that "something exists" is a contingent claim, this "something" means: something other than God. For one might say that the very enterprise Anselm is embarked upon involves showing that "God exists" is not a contingent claim, in which case it would follow that "something exists" is itself not contingent. Gaunilo, however, clearly must assume that something *other than* God exists, and since he offers no argument, we can only take it that he is appealing to what he thought to be obvious (which it is, as a matter of fact). Had he thought that "something exists" was necessarily true, on some philosophical basis, not only might he have offered an argument for it, but he would have been more sympathetic with Anselm's attempt to do this. In actuality, Gaunilo's assumption, taken as it must be as an appeal to the facts, supplies us with a clear indication of how far he was from appreciating the profundity and ingenuity of Anselm's argument.

21. It is worth recalling at this point that the entire line, from which this is taken, reads: "For 'that which is greater than everything' and 'that than which a greater cannot be thought' are not equivalent for the purpose of proving the real existence of the thing spoken of." Charlesworth, p. 179.

22. Charlesworth, p. 180/181.

23. Anselm himself, finally, concludes that: ". . . if what 'that than which a greater cannot be thought' of itself proves concerning itself cannot be proved in the same way in respect of what is said to be 'greater than everything,' you [Gaunilo] criticize me unjustly for having said what I did not say, since it differs so much from what I did say." Charlesworth, p. 181.

24. The only premise that has been questioned as factual, so far as I know, is the one that I have labeled premise 2, which states that "something than which nothing greater can be thought" is understood. If one takes this to mean that some particular Fool understands "something than which nothing greater can be thought" then this may appear to be a factual claim. If, however, we take a hint from the hypothetical character of the Fool, this suspicion can be dismissed. For in this case, we would be reading the premise as claiming that some possible person understands the key phrase; that is, it is possible that "something than which nothing greater can be thought" is understood (by some person). Such an interpretation of this line seems further indicated when we realize that any philosophically interesting criticism of the premise would surely involve showing that the key phrase cannot be understood, and not that it simply does not happen to be understood.

25. And this is the only point in the argument at which Anselm uses *existere* in place of *esse*.

26. Actually, except for the inclusion of *cogitari* ("thought"), the categories Anselm is employing are traditional, dating back to Aristotle.

27. This, of course, is not true in a strictly logical sense, for if something does not exist it follows that it can be thought not to exist. At the same time, to assert this logical "truth" would seem insignificant. The real force of Anselm's claim that something can be thought not to exist only comes through when we are speaking about something that exists.

28. Charlesworth, p. 178/179.

29. Charlesworth, p. 176/177.

30. Here Charlesworth's translation needs to be corrected, for in *Monologion* XXIII and XXIV Anselm distinguishes between *ubique* and *omni loco* and also between *semper* and *omni tempore*, that is, Anselm distinguishes "everywhere" from "in every place" and "always" from "at every time." The general discussion of these and related issues in *Monologion* XVII through XXIV can prove very helpful.

31. Citations of pages referring to this article will come from Alvin Plantinga's *The Ontological Argument*, New York, 1965, pp. 136-159.

32. For example, in his *Anselm's Discovery*, *A Re-examination of the Ontological Proof for God's Existence*, La Salle, Illinois, 1965.

33. Malcolm, p. 140. Great misunderstanding accrues to the sort of account Malcolm gives of II; that is, the traditional account. We have, in treating the *reductio* portion of II as a sub-argument (5a-d, Ch. 1 above), attempted to make clear that what has traditionally been isolated as the crucial matter in II is no such thing (see note 16 above). As a matter of fact, even in rejecting this sub-argument, if the major argu-

ment (the direct demonstration) is sound, all that would follow is that one of its premises (i.e. 5) stands in need of justification. I do not mean to suggest that this is unimportant. But if nothing more than a justification for a premise in an otherwise sound argument is lacking, then it seems the appropriate response is to attempt to provide such a justification, not go off in search of another argument. Anselm himself offers alternative justifications in the replies (especially V and IX) and it is interesting that when he does they are completely modal. Our point in this, as should become evident as we proceed in our discussion of Malcolm, is that if there is a modal argument for the existence of something than which nothing greater can be thought it is in *Proslogion* II and not III, where the interposing of *"cogitari"* in the modal complex (see Henry, *The Logic of St. Anselm*) removes it from any such task. Hartshorne, I believe, has conceded this, and sought his modal argument in the replies.

34. Malcolm, p. 141.

35. Malcolm, p. 142.

36. Henry, in *"Proslogion* Chapter 3" makes the following important claim: "The salient point, and the one that is totally overlooked by most moderns, is that beings which are necessary (i.e. not possible not to be) are, according to the Boethian cosmological background of the commentaries from which Anselm draws his modal logic, comparatively commonplace: one has only to look up into the night sky to see evidence of many such beings. The heavenly bodies provide Boethius with a set of standard examples of necessary beings. Hence to prove that God was a necessary being, or that God necessarily existed would scarcely be a way of exalting God above his creation. Indeed, a creationist metaphysics with this sort of cosmological background tends (as in the case of both Anselm and Aquinas) to make God's aseity, rather than his necessity, the mark of his ontological supremacy. Remarks made by Boethius and Gerbert (cf. *The Logic of St. Anselm* sec. 5. 54) suggest that one reason why *'cogitari'* is inserted, so that 'non potest cogitari non esse' becomes true of God, was to exalt the being of God above that of many created necessary beings which are such that thought *can* decompose them, and which hence, while not possible not to be, can nevertheless be *thought* not to be. The divine simplicity, in contrast, and as is argued in chapters 18 and 22 of *Proslogion*, is unique in resisting the decomposing power of thought. It is this sort of exaltation, rather than any proof for the existence of God based on his being a mere necessary being, which is part of the true point of this chapter 3." (*Analecta Anselmiana* I, p. 103).

37. See Charlesworth, p. 188/189 where Anselm equates "necessarily exists" (*necesse est esse*) with "cannot not exist" (*non possit non esse*).

38. Charlesworth, pp. 178/179-180/181.

39. G. B. Mathews, "On Conceivability in Anselm and Malcolm," *Philosophical Review*, 70, Jan. 1961, pp. 110-111.

40. *Analecta Anselmiana* I, p. 100.

41. This is not so surprising if we recall that the original contained no chapter divisions, in which case the later separation into chapters would not allow for complete disassociation of topics. For Anselm did not rewrite the work into chapters. Rather, he left the text as it stood, placing numbers in the margin which corresponded to a list of chapter headings.

42. La Croix, pp. 23, 24 and 25.

43. La Croix, p. 13, and again p. 35.

44. If Anselm cannot *show* that God is something than which nothing greater can be thought, then the argument is itself based in faith; that "We believe that You are something than which nothing greater can be thought." At some point, Anselm needs to ground this claim in reason. Therefore we cannot simply return to the beginning of II to identify God with something than which nothing greater can be thought, but must wait until this has been shown by argument.

45. Charlesworth, p. 178/179: ". . . proprium est deo non posse cogitari non esse . . ."; ". . . it is the distinguishing characteristic of God that He cannot be thought of as not existing . . . "

46. The importance of the separability or inseparability of II and III from the rest of the *Proslogion* in large measure hinges upon exactly what God one takes Anselm's argument to have shown to exist. In this case, La Croix may be right that the argument of II and III is not sufficient to show that "the being bearing the properties traditionally attributed to God exists" if the properties in question are those of the radically Christian God. At the same time, La Croix does *not* show that even the entire *Proslogion* would be sufficient to demonstrate that. In this way it is important that certain attributes are not entailed by the argument of II and III and have to be, so to speak, affixed to God's being. Triunity would be a good example. Although Anselm later in the text *asserts* that God is triune, he nowhere *argues* for it; nor does it seem to me likely that he would be able to show that triunity is a necessary attribute of the God demonstrated to exist in the argument of II and III. However, with respect to other "traditional attributes" of God, we shall see that many of them are entailed by the "cannot be

thought not to exist"—attributes like immutability, simplicity, etc. So
while some attributes are entailed by the argument, others are not and
often those which might be most significant to a Christian (for example, that his God incarnated). This means that while Anselm's argument does offer a sufficient characterization of this being (than which a
greater cannot be thought) to call it God, it is only the existence of a
being so characterized which the argument can claim to have shown.

47. There is no question that *vere esse* can simply mean "really
exists" and has this use in reference to creatures. What I am claiming
is that when applied to God its signification is more specific.

48. Charlesworth, p. 144/145.

49. For some reason, Charlesworth decided to render *simpliciter* as
"absolute," and one should be aware that he has made this translation
(see the last sentences of the Latin).

50. See above, p. 52.

51. For these "attributes" are all modifiers of God's existence:
that is, God *exists* immutably, simply, absolutely, wholly, etc.

52. *Anselmi Opera Omnia*, vol. I, pp. 45-46, English translation
taken from S. N. Deane, *Basic Writings*, Open Court, 1907, p. 87; *with
crucial alteration*.

53. Schmitt, following Wilmart, who compiled the prayers for the
Critical Edition, does not accept this as an authentic work of Anselm's.
Even in rejecting this meditation, Wilmart has the following to say of its
author: "Med. I—un ouvrage d'Elmer, moine de avait justemente
observé, dams cette "méditation" des traits qui paraissent aussi chez
saint Anselme, notamnent dans le *Monologion* et le *Proslogion*. Elmer,
en effect, a dû connaître personnellement l'archevêque et subir son
influence; en bon disciple, il l'a imité." Wilmart, A., *Autheurs spirituels
et textes dévots du moyen âge latin*, Paris, 1932, p. 193. So even
though Wilmart rejects the meditation, he accepts that it has all the
characteristics of an original, indeed, that, as we shall see, it is strikingly
like two of Anselm's other works. He explains this likeness by noting
that the author of this passage knew Anselm personally, fell under his
influence, and as a good disciple, imitated him. This constitutes enough
of a connection with Anselm to give the meditation serious attention.

54. J. P. Migne, *Patrologia Latina*, v. 148, p. 712.

55. A. Stolz, " '*Vere esse*' im *Proslogion* des hl. Anselm",
Scholastik, vol. 9, 1934. In this crucial article Stolz shows that *vere
esse* had been used by the tradition leading up to Anselm to refer to
God alone, that is, this phrase had a special meaning, for example, in
Augustine. This is significant, for it is well-known (see Preface to
Monologion) that Anselm strove to be consistent with "the writings of

the Catholic Fathers, and *especially* those of St. Augustine." Numerous references to and quotes from Augustine demonstrate that: "Vere esse bezeichnet also für Augustine das absolute, unveränderliche, göttliche Sein." (p. 403) And commenting of Exodus 3. 14: "Ego sum qui sum," Augustine says: "Est enim vere solus, quia incommutabilis est . . . " (Stolz, p. 403). From this, Stolz concludes: " . . . *Proslogion 3 befasst sich ja sicher nicht mit der einfachen Existenz Gottes, sondern ausschliesslich mit seiner besondern Seinsweise.*" (p. 409).

56. We will have a chance to see Anselm develop this point during our inspection of *Proslogion* IV.

57. Charlesworth is himself forced to render *quomodo* as "in what sense" in a reply in which Anselm says: "Quomodo tamen dicatur cogitari deus non esse, in ipso libello puto sufficienter esse dictum," which he translates: "In what sense, however, God can be thought of as not existing I think I have adequately explained in my tract." (p. 178/179).

58. See "Wort und Wirklichkeit bei Anselm von Canterbury," V. Warnach, in *Saltzburger Jahrbuch für Philosophie*, 5/6, 1961/62, pp. 157-177.

59. *Anselmi Opera Omnia*, vol. I, pp. 24-25, English translation taken from Deane, pp. 56-57; with alteration.

60. If we are to understand this, then we must be clear that when Anselm speaks of "imagination" he is *not* referring to the power of free fancy, which is presumed to invent independent of reality (of "the things themselves"). Rather, imagination signifies quite literally the power of the mind to entertain bodily images, all of which have their source externally. On this account, what we ordinarily call imagination is the re-ordering and re-uniting of these primary sensory images (see *Monologion* XI).

61. Augustine refers (*De Trin.*, XV, 20; and 10, 19; 15, 25) to this "inner word" as "verbum quod in corde (vel mente) dicimus"; "the word which we say in the heart (or mind)," while Anselm concludes *Monologion* X claiming that " . . . non immerito videri potest apud summam substantiam, talem rerum locutionem et fuisse antequam essent ut per eam fierent, et esse cum facta sunt ut per eam sciantur"; " . . . not without reason it may be thought that such an expression of things existed with the supreme substance before their creation, that they might be created; and exists, now that they have been created, that they may be known through it." (*Anselmi Opera Omnia*, vol. I, p. 25; Deane, p. 58). This is, shall we say, the metaphysical ground out of which the illumination theory of knowledge grows.

62. See *Monologion* LXVI.

63. In *Epistola de Incarnatione Verbi* I, Anselm suggests this distinction is so fundamental, that those who cannot make it ought to be excluded from any discussion of spiritual questions: "In eorum quippe animabus ratio, quae et princeps et iudex debet omnium esse quae sunt in homine, sic est in imaginationibus corporalibus obvoluta, ut ex eis se non possit evolvere, nec ab ipsis ea quae ipsa sola et pura contemplare debet, valeat discernere." (*Anselmi Opera Omnia*, vol. II, p. 10) Fairweather translates this: "For their soul's reason, which should be the chief and judge of everything in man, is so muffled up in corporeal imaginings that it cannot unroll itself from them, nor is it able to distinguish from them the things it ought to contemplate pure and unadulterated." (in *A Scholastic Miscellany*, Philadelphia, 1956, p. 99).

64. *Anselmi Opera Omnia*, vol. I, pp. 93-94, where it seems to me indicated that the sole purpose of writing these works and circulating them among the brethren was to assist the monks with their meditation. In this connection, I might mention that the account I am offering here should serve to fill out the significance of the "withdrawal from the world" characteristic of monasticism.

65. To this extent, Anselm is already hinting his answer to the question posed at the conclusion of III in the way in which that question is put. For he asks how the Fool can say that God does not exist when it is "evident to a rational mind" (*in promptu sit rationali menti*) that God cannot be thought not to exist. The answer is, put simply, that the Fool has not practiced the use of his "rational mind" and so matters such as these have never been properly visible (*promptus*) to him.

66. In *Epistola de Incarnatione Verbi* VI we are told that the purpose of both the *Monologion* and *Proslogion* was: " . . . ad respondendem pro fide contra eos, qui nolentes credere quod non intelligunt derident credentes, sive ad adiuvandum religiosum studium eorum qui humiliter quaerunt intelligere quod firmissime eredunt . . . " (*Anselmi Opera Omnia*, vol. II, p. 21); "to answer, on behalf of our faith, those who, while unwilling themselves to believe whay they do not understand, deride others who do believe. And . . . to assist the conscientious striving of those who seek humbly to understand what they already firmly believe." Translation taken from J. Hopkins and H. Richardson: *Trinity, Incarnation, and Redemption: Theological Treatises*, New York, 1970, p. 21. Notice that the aim is to "answer" the fools and to "assist" the faithful, but on no account to convince anyone of anything.

67. Charlesworth, p. 114/115.

68. I have already mentioned in note 4 that Barth holds the view as

stated in this paragraph, and that Henry holds a variant of it. It should now be clear that although La Croix does not want to break up the *Proslogion* into any parts, that is, he wants to treat it all as a single argument, he nonetheless succeeds in separating II and III from the rest of the work as dealing with a series of existential deductions, while V-XXVI are treated as attempts to show that all the attributes traditionally attributed to God belong to something than which nothing greater can be thought. This is, in essence, to agree with Barth's division of the text.

69. This is Stolz's reading.

70 In what follows, the Latin of *Proslogion* I will be taken from Schmitt's presentation of it in his translation of the *Proslogion*, Stuttgart-Bad Cannstatt, 1961. We will continue to take the English translation from Charlesworth, with alteration.

71. As it seems Stolz would have it. See the introduction to his *Anselm von Canterbury*, Munich, 1937.

72. The nature of argument so understood can be succinctly characterized by noting that *"arguo"* roots in a Greek word (ἀργός) meaning bright, and therefore has as its primary signification the sense of to bring into clear or bright light; that is, to illuminate.

73. *Anselmi Opera Omnia*, vol. I, p. 76; Deane, pp. 129-130.

74. There can be no doubt that flawed reasoning may sever the attempt to provide intuitive vision. It is, however, as surely the case that the intuition of God is, in some sense, separable from the discursive reasoning. Boldly put, the intuitive dimension of an argument may be satisfied even if the discursive dimension is in some degree wanting. Were this not the case, one could never "correct" an argument. For such correction (even by the author) is the result, when it is really the correction of the original argument, of gaining the intuitive results from a piece of reasoning which nonetheless may allow for discursive improvements. In fact, it seems to me, the history of the development of the so-called ontological argument is nothing but this sort of discursive correction; that is, the same intuitive insight resides at the heart of all such arguments, although each thinker develops a discursive "argument" he hopes more amenable to that intuition. In this way, an evaluation of the discursive aspect of Anselm's argument, although it may be of some value, is really a secondary matter. The crucial element of evaluation must center about its intuitive claim.

Index